TRADING CHICAGO STYLE

TRADING CHICAGO STYLE

INSIGHTS AND STRATEGIES OF TODAY'S TOP TRADERS

NEAL T. WEINTRAUB

McGraw-Hill
New York   San Francisco   Washington, D.C.   Auckland
Bogotá   Caracas   Lisbon   London   Madrid   Mexico City
Milan   Montreal   New Delhi   San Juan   Singapore
Sydney   Tokyo   Toronto

Library of Congress Cataloging-in-Publication Data

Weintraub, Neal.
    Trading Chicago style / by Neal Weintraub.
      p.   cm.
    ISBN 0-07-069632-2
    1. Commodity exchanges.   2. Commodity futures.   3. Futures.
  I. Title.
HG6046.W44   1999
332.64'273—dc21   99-53531
                                         CIP

McGraw-Hill

*A Division of The **McGraw·Hill** Companies*

1 2 3 4 5 6 7 8 9 0 DOC/DOC 9 0 9 8 7 6 5 4 3 2 1 0 9

ISBN 0-07-069632-2

Printed and bound by R. R. Donnelley & Sons Company.

This publication is designed to provide accurate and authoritative information in regard to the subject matter covered. It is sold with the understanding that neither the author nor the publisher is engaged in rendering legal, accounting, or other professional service. If legal advice or other expert assistance is required, the services of a competent professional person should be sought.

    —From a Declaration of Principles jointly adopted by a Committee of the American Bar Association and a Committee of Publishers.

McGraw-Hill books are available at special quantity discounts to use as premiums and sales promotions, or for use in corporate training programs. For more information, please write to the Director of Special Sales, McGraw-Hill, 11 West 19th Street, New York, NY 10011. Or contact your local bookstore.

This book is printed on recycled, acid-free paper containing a minimum of 50% recycled de-inked fiber.

CONTENTS

PREFACE

If you are seeking a book about trading, written by celebrities, do not purchase this book. If, however, you are seeking concrete, solid information and knowledge from traders, rsearchers, and other interesting and talented individuals, you've come to the right place. For years now, I have noticed a disparity between real traders and "gurus," who appeal to the public speculator. *Trading Chicago Style: Insights and Strategies of Today's Top Traders,* is a follow-up and in-depth exploration of many of the topics outlined in my previous book, *Tricks of the Floor Trader.* When I mention trading Chicago style, people think of the raucous cacophony of the trading pits. But it is more than that. It is a style of trading going back to before the Civil War. It is trading characterized by huge liquid markets and market makers prepared to make a fair trade in all kinds of volatile market conditions.

Trading Chicago Style is more than a look at pit trading. As Chicago markets have evolved, pit trading has already reached critical mass. Certainly, electronic technology in trading is the next logical step.

Many of the names in this book you may not recognize. I find there is an inverse relationship between celebrity status and trading success. Each person in this book was interviewed by me in Chicago. In some cases I went back three, four, and even five times to extract relevant, cogent information.

As you read *Trading Chicago Style,* you will find various opinions on systems versus intuition, or back-testing versus experience. That will be fun and informative reading. Equally important, in my estimation, are the common threads of money management, risk adversity, and psychology that permeate *Trading Chicago Style.*

ACKNOWLEDGMENTS

No one can attempt to write a book without support and assistance. It is unfortunate that books cannot have closing credits as do Hollywood movies. Why, even the caterer for the extras gets a credit.

While I cannot go that far, I certainly owe a debt of gratitude to my parents and my nieces, Lynn and Laura, who wonder exactly what I do. Also, a "thank you" to Elise Richter, who is convinced I was dating when I was not answering the phone. And I certainly owe thanks to Stormy Enterprises for typing and logistical support.

Believe it or not, I also wish to thank my adversaries. They earn more money on trader gullibility than trading the markets. They provided the motivation for *Trading Chicago Style* by promoting rags-to-riches courses, at-home back-testing, magic indicators, trademarked indicators, seasonals, Wally World seminars, and excessive day-trading.

In this age of media tonnage, where advertising is disguised as truth, it's hoped this "little voice" finds you.

Finally, thanks to Keller Graduate School and the Educational Department of the Chicago Mercantile Exchange (www.cme.com). (They have great courses.)

TRADING CHICAGO STYLE

DR. SID KAZ

Training the Floor Trader

Sid was the first person to introduce me to trading Chicago style. Despite what people think, Sid was not in the "Board of Trade Civil War Brigade." However, his Ph.D. in education and understanding of human behavior is why Sid trains traders.

Neal: When I say "trading Chicago style," what pops into your mind?

Sid: Well, of course, it's the crowded pits, the waving of arms and shouting, a lot of excitement on the floor. You can feel the electricity in the room—it's floor trading.

Neal: Is it fair to say you've trained more people to trade Chicago style than just about anybody else in Chicago?

Sid: I would say that I'm probably up there with most, but you have to remember that no other firm—that I know of—has made a commitment to provide an ongoing program to train floor traders. I started my career with SMW Trading back in 1984, and I was assisting the partners of the firm in training traders. After about two years, they stopped running the trading program and turned it over to me. I did have the advantage of

1

having been a floor trader for five years, as well as a teacher, coach, and high school principal. So you see, it was just like being back in the classroom or out on the football field for me.

Neal: Many of the people I've traded with on the floor have been trained by you. As a matter of fact, we affectionately refer to them as "Sid's kids." How many people do you think you've trained—ballpark?

Sid: It's hard to come up with a number, because I've never thought about it. Maybe six or seven hundred. I don't know.

Neal: In a year how many people go through your trading program?

Sid: It fluctuates because it's an ongoing program of people who are either attempting to get into the industry or would like an introduction to it.

Neal: Why are you the best kept secret outside of Chicago? Nobody knows that if you want to become a Chicago floor trader, your firm has a training program and helps people get started. Is it kind of a closed society thing? Why don't you folks advertise, let people know?

Sid: You are right. We have not done a good job of advertising that we provide the best training program for local floor traders. We have started a more rigorous campaign on the Internet. We are also looking at the print media to get the word out.

Neal: When I took your classes, you observed me—how I did mock trading. In seeing how I did, you would then decide if I might be the kind of local you would want to have. Is that still the essence of what you're doing?

Sid: Pretty much so, as long as the person doesn't come in undercapitalized. Now, there are a number of firms that will take people with a minimal amount of capitalization, allow them to trade, charge them a hefty commission on each trade, and provide them with no support service. We don't do that. We take a very personal interest in our traders. We want a person to be able to go on the floor and have the best possible opportunity to succeed. If people come in with a minimal amount of money, one of two things is going to happen. Either they are going to take unnecessary or inappropriate risks or they won't do anything, and in order to succeed on the floor, you have to trade. It's okay to start out at 3, 4, 5, 8, 10, 12 contracts a day, but eventually, you must build volume.

Neal: Volume would be what? How many contracts?

Sid: It depends on the pit where the person is trading. If somebody is starting in the bond pit, let's say, our goal is to get them to trade 20 to 40 contracts a day, and scratch them all for a two-week period. We want them to learn to get in and out of the market, to trade as unemotionally as possible, to get to the point that they're on automatic pilot.

Neal: They don't even have to think?

Sid: It's more than thinking. It has to do with ego. It's working to take the emotion out of your trading. It's learning that not every trade will make money. It's knowing how to deal with a loss.

Neal: That reminds me of one time in your training program when you grabbed me by the shoulder and said, "Stop thinking, just do it!"

Sid: Right, because we don't have a crystal ball. Our goal is to let the market tell us what it wants to do. Our trading philoso-

phy begins with learning how to be a defensive trader before going onto offense. We want to prevent you from losing money.
We look at a scratch trade as a winning trade. Ninety-five percent of the people on the floor, if they're bidding 11 and somebody sells them 1 at 11, are going to immediately offer it at 12 or
hold onto it thinking they are going to make 100 ticks on that
one trade. That isn't what we try to get our traders to do.

**Neal: So if I buy at 11 and the market does not go to 12
immediately, I'm going to scratch the trade immediately?**

Sid: Immediately. The basic point I'm trying to make is that we
really focus on a person learning to be an effective trader. So
when the day comes that you buy it at 11 and it goes 12 bid, we
want you to sell it immediately and take your profit. We focus on
this approach until trainees show that they're capable of handling themselves in the pit without losing large sums of money.

Neal: Okay, so that would be called stage one?

Sid: Stage one.

Neal: How long would stage one last?

Sid: Stage one depends on the person's performance. We set a
goal. We say our goal is to get you to 20 to 40 contracts a day.
Now, that may work in the bond pit, but we have a lot of new
traders who are trading in the MidAm grains. If you're able to
get up to 5, your goal is to go to 10, again, to just scratch the
trades. I'm 95% convinced that you can scratch trades in any
market if you don't let your ego get in the way. Let's say you've
made three or four trades on a given day and you've scratched
them all. You may be up one tick and all of a sudden in the next
trade, the market goes against you. You don't want to go home

and say, "I did not make money." That's letting your ego get in the way. So you let the market go against you, and instead of losing one tick, you lose more.

Neal: So let's say my trading assistant, Duncan, goes through the first six months; he scratches all of his trades; he's gone the distance. Now he's wondering, "Okay, Sid, what's stage two?"

Sid: He's been trading one at a time. Now we say, "Here's what you do, Duncan. When you bid 11 and somebody hits you at 11, you offer it at 12 twice. If nobody buys it, you scratch the trade." You offer it only twice. That's stage two. Now let's say that you've offered it once or twice and somebody buys it. You've made some money—fine, no problem. What's the next stage? You bid for two contracts. When somebody sells you the two contracts, you scratch one right away and offer one at 12 twice. If nobody buys it, scratch it at 11 again. So it's a progression. We want a person to learn to trade one contract successfully. Then you can move to two lots, then to three lots, then to five lots, but always getting out of part of it. After that, you might move up to another stage where you do five lots. You might scratch two; offer two, once . . . twice, get out of them; offer one more, somebody buys it and you go on. So it's a stacked progression. Each person travels through these stages on an individual basis. There is no way to predict. Through the seminars I've found people who have been able to master the mechanical and psychological concepts. I tell them, "When you go on the floor, you're going to be the very best prepared new trader. However, you're still an amateur playing against the pros. You've got to work to become a pro." We feel comfortable that after attending our classes, a person can go to the floor, let's say 8 or 10 times, without the fear of being blown out of the water.

Neal: Is fear a factor?

Sid: There's fear for some people, yes.

Neal: Sid, stage three, that is your graduation?

Sid: Yes.

Neal: How many contracts a day are some of your big traders doing now?

Sid: We have some very good traders down there. They'll do hundreds, two hundred, five hundred. But the thing is, many of them still scratch 70 to 80% of their trades.

Neal: What's amazing is that the public thinks we are making money every day and not scratching at all.

Sid: That's a common misconception. The reason is that the public hears about the 5% who've become extremely successful. They do not focus on the other 95%. This industry does have a high turnover. It has been said that there is approximately a 75% turnover every two to three years. We've been very fortunate. Because of our training, we have had a much higher success ratio. When I meet with people who come to our firm, I explain that we do have a philosophy of trading. Now, if you want to be a position trader and clear through our firm, we can do that, but you need more money in your account for margining purposes. Because if you put a 5-lot on and you only have $5000 in your account, imagine what's going to happen. We've lived through limit moves, so we know what it's like. A guy off the street doesn't understand that. He's never been caught in a market long when it's limit down for two days in a row.

Neal: What are some of the characteristics, qualities, and background you look for in a person?

Sid: There is really no academic preparation that would prepare you for trading on the floor. Undoubtedly, there are people here on the floor who graduated high school, put in a couple years of college, came down here as runners, and ultimately became successful. There may be some people with Ph.D.s who turned out to be lousy floor traders because they tried to think too much.

Neal: Well, Sid, let's not go too hard on the thinkers out there.

Sid: I'm not rubbing it in, it's just a fact: traders who want to use their academic or intellectual skills of trading will follow a different style of trading. We do not know how to predict where the market is going. There are hundreds of different systems, but at one time or another they will all be affected by what has been called "chaos theory." It's a different style; that's all it is. We feel we have a unique operation, and we're real good at training floor traders. So we stay with our strengths.

Neal: So, you take people, give them a chance, watch them in the mock trading, and see if they get it.

Sid: In the course of the past 14 years, I can count on one hand the number of people who, after two or three months in our training, had to be told they ought to rethink whether floor trading was for them. I've done that only when the person came in with, let's say, $25,000 to risk, part of his retirement fund or money borrowed on his home. I'd say, "You've worked too hard to get where you're at. The money you need for floor trading you've got to be able to risk. If you think you can come in with $5000 or $10,000 and turn it into $100,000, you're sadly mistaken."

Neal: But we've seen books where guys have said they've turned $10,000 into $1,000,000 and they're off-the-floor traders.

Sid: Yes, you're right. You're talking about how many Michael Jordans, Scotty Pippens, and Joe Montanas of trading? There are such people, but what about the people you don't hear about? They fold up their tents and move away because they've lost it all. People who want to trade off the floor need to be watching every single market, whether it's gold, sugar, cocoa, orange juice, crude, soybeans, or Swiss francs, because you're always looking for that market that's making a breakout. You can't do that by limiting yourself to watching the bonds or the S&Ps because all the contracts trade in a trading range until they move up or down with a major move.

Neal: You're absolutely right.

Sid: Coming back to the question you asked about the characteristics of a trader. I think it has to be the kind of person who has a degree of self-assuredness, but not arrogance. The market will always make you pay if you come in with arrogance. We all talk about being disciplined, but you really test your mettle on the floor and discover if you're really disciplined. Another characteristic, and I will describe it politely, is this: If you buy into your own b.s. or excuses, you won't succeed. The floor doesn't let you make excuses. "Because the broker jammed me," "I couldn't get out," "I lost my count"—these are all excuses. You can always get out. Those who say otherwise are just unwilling to pay up, unwilling to take the loss. Their egos won't allow it. Or you play a game with yourself: "I swear, if it goes down one more tick, I'll get out."

Neal: Like the floor went for my stops.

Sid: Right. People want to be right, and they want to make the market wrong.

Neal: Is it possible to have a losing day and still call yourself a good trader?

Sid: Absolutely.

Neal: So if I were to hold onto a trade beyond the point that I told myself I would and it paid off, that would be merely a lucky trade, whereas if I had gotten out of it when I should have with a loss, I would have been a better trader because my discipline would eventually catch me a streak.

Sid: Exactly. And as you begin to become more sensitive to the nuances of the pit, more able to see and hear what's going on, and more able to take your emotions out of it, then you will be able to build the base you need to be successful. Some of the best days I've had were days when I would be down 20 ticks and at the end of the day just be down two. I consider that a very good day.

Neal: Is there any one book on floor trading that you would recommend to the reader?

Sid: I really can't recommend any specific book. This is experiential. It has to do with your emotions, your personal makeup, and being truly disciplined.

Neal: So if I want to become a Chicago floor trader, I just better put my shirt and pants on and come to Chicago and talk to you?

Sid: Yes.

Neal: Who's the oldest trader on the floor who's been through your training program and said, "I want to do this."

Sid: We've got a gentleman trading in one of the pits who is in his late fifties or early sixties. Now I'm not saying he's setting the world on fire, but I have said to people, "If you have the opportunity and the economic wherewithal, you don't want to look back five years from now and say, 'Gee, why didn't I do that when I had the opportunity.'" If you can afford what it takes financially, psychologically, and emotionally to give yourself that year to come down here and try it, I encourage anyone. If you don't succeed, at least you seized the opportunity to follow your dream.

Neal: I have so many people who call me and say, "I want to become a trader." My usual reply is, "Great, when can I expect you?" Yet out of every 100 calls, maybe 5 actually come to Chicago and make that commitment.

Sid: It's a big commitment.

Neal: These people keep dreaming, saying to themselves, "What if? What if?" The years go by so fast, and they end up losing their jobs somewhere. What I like about this business is that nobody's going to tell you to retire.

Sid: That's right.

Neal: Nobody's going to say, "I'm sorry, we didn't like your memo. You have to leave."

Sid: Right.

Neal: Or, "We're downsizing, you're out of here."

Sid: You are your own boss. You make all of the decisions. Now, some people are afraid to make decisions. It's like that book *Escape to Freedom*, by, I think it was, Eric Fromm. It's about people not liking to make decisions. They would rather have somebody impose it on them. Then they have the outlook that "so-and-so made me do it." They don't want to take responsibility. So I would look for books on how to learn to take care of your own emotions. Because 95% of trading is emotional.

Neal: Duncan and I just came from the Ceres Cafe. We were wandering around looking for you.

Sid: (laughing) Not during the trading day.

Neal: It's really sad. You see guys down there at 10:15 a.m. drinking gin and tonic.

Sid: Well, you know, one of our very best locals has a philosophy, "During the week, I never touch alcohol." We tell our employees, "We can't dictate your private life, but if you're in a bar at 11 or 12 o'clock at night and you have to be on the floor by 7:20 a.m. tomorrow and you've got a little buzz on, you're not going to be functioning as a pro. You're going to be an amateur, and you're going to lose money." This is a very demanding business, physically and emotionally, and you've got to make yourself as totally ready as you can.

Neal: So, people can ask for you and you'll give them the information on how to get into the trading program?

Sid: Yes.

Neal: As an example, what pits would you recommend for Duncan here?

Sid: I would have to say to Duncan, or anyone else like him, to first come to a couple of sessions of the seminar to see how quickly he picks things up.

Neal: You've just given me an idea, Sid. When is your next seminar?

Sid: Tomorrow.

Neal: Duncan, would you like to watch? (Duncan Robinson was my trading assistant for that quarter. He is a graduate of Indiana University and is currently an options trader.)

Duncan: Sure. I'd love to.

Sid: I think another dimension has to do with the financial situation of the person. We have quite a few of our newer traders trading in the MidAm. I tell people that the MidAm is like AA ball. It's a step up from the seminars. Real money is at risk. However, there are some inherent difficulties with that market. You can't buy a membership for $10,000 and think you've bought a $500,000 membership or a $675,000 membership, but it is a great place to learn to trade. On the other hand, let's say Duncan came to me and said, "I've been very fortunate. I've always wanted to trade. I've got this $250,000 inheritance and I've always wanted to trade S&Ps." I would explain to him the exchange requirements, the rent of a membership, and I would start him on an intensive training program. Some people say, "Well, what about night bond trading?" We've never had anyone who has succeeded at trading night bonds. My fear is that a person will learn bad habits, and I would rather not have a person trade in a market where there is opportunity to learn bad habits.

Neal: Just as an aside, in my last book, I wrote about a character called "the Vampire." He went through your training program. He was a MidAm bond trader. He now has a yellow badge. The Vampire only trades at night. The skills that he has learned—that you taught him as a floor trader—foremost of which is the ability to scalp, make him an excellent living trading with a computer. I

think it's fascinating that the on-the-floor skills you taught him help him to trade off the floor.

Sid: Thank you.

Neal: Sid, you talk a lot about discipline. Can you incorporate money management into your philosophy, or is that a separate issue when you talk to young traders?

Sid: I think it's more of a separate issue because we're starting with someone who might be a brand-new trader, but the discipline leads to money management. As a matter of fact, that's really what we're doing, trying to help you manage your money by not giving it back. If you come in with $50,000 and every trade you make, you lose 5 or 10 ticks, you have to ask why. We want you to look at what's going on. Why are you losing this kind of money? That would be part of money management: learning to take the small loss and learning to take the small profit, at least until you become more professional.

Neal: I think one of the reasons your firm is so successful is that your traders know that they have to answer to you at the end of the day. There are no excuses, unlike many of the public traders I know.

Sid: That's one of the strengths of SMW. We really do take a personal interest in our traders. When people are doing poorly, we want to meet with them and try to help them. I do everything I was trained to do—as a coach, as a principal, and as a counselor. A lot of times, talking with traders, going over what they're doing, gives them the psychological boost they need to get over the bad periods that do occur.

Neal: So you will help people lease a seat?

Sid: Yes.

Neal: Buy a seat?

Sid: Yes.

Neal: You'll get them trained, you'll put them on the floor, and if you do not feel that they qualify for your program, you'll turn them on to other firms?

Sid: It's not that a person doesn't qualify for our program. Rather, I might call a trader in to talk with me, and I'll say, "At this point, in comparison to other people who've been trading as long as you have in a similar kind of pit, you're down toward the bottom quarter of the class. I think you need to take a look at what you're doing, and by the way, you may need to put $5000 or $10,000 more into your account." I rarely ask anybody to leave. People I've asked to leave have been those who've totally disregarded what we were saying.

Neal: Now, I don't want everyone to think all of your people are 5- or 10-lot traders, but you've got some pretty serious folks out there. You've got traders doing a couple thousand a day.

Sid: In some cases, even more.

Neal: Some of these traders are the ones you don't read about, because they don't want their names known. They don't want to do the seminar circuit. They don't want anyone to know what they're doing.

Sid: Exactly. To keep a low profile, I think, is an asset.

Neal: Are there any other firms you know of that offer training programs?

Sid: To be honest with you, I know of no firm that offers a bona fide training program. I do know the exchanges run seminars on simulated trading techniques, but their programs are for a short duration, lack follow-through, and do not provide anyone who will be available to talk to a trader. I know of no other firm that has made this support available. We encourage the people who come to our seminars to keep coming, it's the kind of thing they can keep coming back to in order to improve their performance.

Neal: Is your program free?

Sid: No, we've recently instituted a $250 fee. This is a one-time charge. If a person comes to several seminars, I am happy to provide her or him with as much individual attention as is needed. But we need a commitment. I have received letters from people who have attended our seminars in the past who said that the fee was the best $250 they had spent. It either gave them the skills they needed to succeed or made them realize that floor trading wasn't for them. In some cases it prevented them from making a potentially greater, more costly, mistake.

Neal: If people want to contact you, will you welcome inquiries?

Sid: Any time. Our phone number is (312) 913-6100.

Neal: Sid, thanks.

Sid: You're very welcome. I've enjoyed it.

Neal: I also want to thank Duncan Robinson.

Here is an e-mail I received from Timothy Morge about the interview with Sid Kaz.

Neal,

This interview does a great job of capturing the essence of learning to be a successful floor trader. (I know. I held a seat for 6 long months in 1995, and I quickly learned that the ego I had developed from being a successful off-floor trader kept me from developing into a successful floor trader.) Having read this interview, I wish I had known about the program. I truly would have tried it.

Although I dabbled with trading silver and gold during college, I learned to trade as a market maker in the cash currency markets beginning in 1980. Those next five or six years were great times to be a market maker, and now that I've read the interview, I can tell you the skills needed to be a great market maker in the cash currencies, when they are as actively traded bank to bank as they were then, are the same skills you'd learn and utilize as a floor trader. Before I left the bank world in 1990, I probably taught over 100 traders to be competent market makers, and one of the difficult skills to teach was keeping only the position you wanted. At a top volume bank, I was making 500 trades a day and turning over near $8 billion US. Other banks were calling in constantly, so I'd have three to five other traders answering phones and relaying my two-sided price, then telling me if I just bought or sold $5 million US or more on each price. If someone dealt on my price, I'd shade my next price accordingly. If they passed, I'd have someone getting me a two-way price back, so I could dump what I didn't want—or I would turn the position in the cash brokers or on the IMM floor.

As you pointed out in the interview, it's the dealing without thinking part that cannot break down. Although I might turn over $8 billion US in a day, I probably never kept positions that averaged more than $50 million US in either direction at one time, and the key to making money was the ability to turn volume over and over and over, making a pip here and there on all of those turns. But if you begin thinking you actually *know* where it's all going to go while being a market maker, you are in serious trouble.

Well, that was my life as a market maker. I am a trader now, a speculator. Quite a different exercise. But your interview with the good doctor was quite informative and spot-on.

Thanks for letting me read it.

Tim

Note: Timothy Morge can be contacted at: tmorge@interaccess. com.

PIT STOPS

BLACK AND SCHOLES MAKE A NAME

Black and Scholes made their names with the Black-Scholes formula, a method of pricing options that was first published in 1973 in the University of Chicago's *Journal of Political Economy*. Just one month before the formula's publication, the Chicago Board of Options Exchange had opened, providing the first formula market for options trading.

Options give investors the opportunity, but not the obligation, to buy or sell assets at a prespecified price. Until the Black-Scholes formula, investors in share options, futures, and other derivative securities—called derivatives because their worth is affected by, or derived from, fluctuations in the value of other assets—could not be sure of the value of their securities. Many researchers tried to determine the value with formulas that required assigning risk premiums. Black and Scholes realized that a stock's price already reflected the options risk and devised their famous formula accordingly.

In the past quarter century, the options market has exploded, with the Black-Scholes formula awarded much of the credit. In the first nine months of 1997, the *Wall Street Journal* reported, the value of U.S. exchange-traded options reached $155 billion.

"Nowadays, thousands of traders and investors use the formula every day to value stock options in markets throughout the world," wrote the Nobel committee. "Such rapid and widespread application of a theoretical result was new to economics."

Merton Miller, who influenced the work of Black and Scholes and published his own article on option valuation in 1973, generalized the formula, taking it beyond options on shares and applying it to other derivatives. The Black-Merton-Scholes methodology has been used, for example, to design optimal financial contracts and to determine values of insurance contracts and guarantees.

Though best known for his work in options, Scholes has also studied the effects of dividends on share prices and has researched the effects of global tax policies on decision making.

NINA COOPER

You Gotta Know Elliott

Nina Cooper is an instructor at the Chicago Mercantile Exchange. She teaches an advanced technical analysis course, Elliott Wave Theory, which is based on the concept of cycles within cycles. As a powerful nonlinear forecasting technique, Elliott Wave Theory can be applied using any time horizon, from tick charts to long-term weekly and monthly data. I first met Ms. Cooper while attending a Market Technician meeting in Chicago.

I invited her to speak to my trading classes at DePaul University. Currently, Nina is president of the Market Technicians Association. This luncheon interview was done prior to her assuming that position.

Neal: Interviewing a friend seems so awkward, but this is the first time we've had the chance to chat for a long time. I just got done listening to a CNBC broadcast, and all they talked about were "good buying recommendations."

Nina: Of course, I think there is probably a bias toward being long. Most people who are nonprofessionals are more inclined to ask where they can buy and aren't thinking in terms of taking a short position.

Neal: Some software gurus say you can't predict the market direction.

Nina: There are ways of knowing where the market is going. An accurate answer to that question is a function of how much time and effort you're willing to put in. There are ways to determine how markets are going to move, and if you're willing to do the work, you can be very accurate indeed. So I would disagree and would take the other side and say *yes,* you can tell where the markets are going.

Neal: With what kind of time frame?

Nina: It doesn't make any difference what kind of time frame. I'll explain that. I do a lot of work with Elliott Wave, which is a sophisticated way of looking at cycles. Using cycles can be a remarkably accurate technique to determine where things are going, in any number of time frames.

Neal: People say that we're entering a new era of economics. The old days don't mean anything. It's a whole new world. Can you explain some of the major cycles that have occurred?

Nina: Well, the classic statement is, "It's different this time." In fact, it really isn't. It's just that the details change a bit. Markets are driven by psychology. Underlying this is a sort of lemminglike shift from one side of the spectrum to the other, from being very optimistic to being very pessimistic. And individuals' decisions made along the way tend to reflect the level of optimism at a particular point in time. So it's never different. It's always a variation of what's happened before.

Neal: So it's like your son or daughter saying, "Mom, you don't know what it's like to be in love. It's different for us. You've never felt this way."

Nina: We've all been there, one time or another.

Neal: We've had some major events this century. We had the 1929 stock market crash. In previous centuries we had the "tulip mania" in the 1600s. We had the cycle of the 1890s. This bull market has seemed to fool everybody.

Nina: Yes.

Neal: It's even fooled Mr. (Bob) Prechter down there in Georgia, hasn't it? Is he part of the Elliott Wave school?

Nina: Bob is probably the foremost of those living who are carrying the Elliott story forward. He has played an enormous role in making Elliott's ideas known to a whole new generation of people in the marketplace.

Neal: He seems to get considerable publicity.

Nina: He has been wrong at times, there's no doubt about it. He has been the first to admit to that. I would hesitate to try to explain why, because it would be utterly presumptuous of me. What I do know is that Bob sees a very significant change on the horizon. He has been aware of its approach for a very long time. And just like a person standing in a station waiting for the train to come through, you think you see it a lot of times before it actually shows up. The situation is much the same in the markets, in the economy in general; it's sort of an analogy. Bob's been looking for something that he knows is coming, and he has seen early signs of it, but he's been early. It hasn't happened yet. It's possible that it's in progress now.

Neal: Right! That's happened many times, even in the 1929 market crash. I'll have to check my history. There

were so many articles written trying to warn the public. Even the Federal Reserve knew it was coming, and they warned some of their key investors.

Nina: Yes, that's interesting.

Neal: All I am suggesting is that once the crash was coming, people saw a way to take advantage of it. One such person was Jesse Livermore. Getting back to the subject, do you have clients now who subscribe to your services?

Nina: Yes.

Neal: Tell me about your services.

Nina: I write a daily commentary on U.S. interest rates and some currencies in the cash market. I look at benchmark 10-year and 30-year issues. My clients are very much involved in the Canadian interest rate market as well. Prior to starting this business, I worked for the Bank of Montreal. Before that, I managed a multicurrency bond portfolio in London. The dollar bloc markets were my specialty, and the Canadian market was an important part of my focus.

Neal: Elliott Wave plays a large part in your work. How significant is it?

Nina: The thing about Elliott that's really misunderstood is that it's a system. By that I mean it's a framework that allows you to look at the market on any time horizon and evaluate what's going on. Using Elliott principles, you can look at very long term data and make a long-term forecast. But at the other extreme, you can use short-term data—tick charts if you choose—and work on a very short intraday view. You can use it in any setting.

In my mind it carries more weight than a lot of traditional technical tools, because it encompasses everything going on in the market at any point in time.

Neal: Elliott has been accused of being more of an art than an indicator.

Nina: I would agree with you. That is a legitimate criticism. I've been working with Elliott for quite a long time. It's not so much that Elliott is complicated; it's that it requires a different way of approaching price data. It means you have to use logic, unravel a set of clues to come up with an answer, and many find that takes more work than they're prepared to do. However, I've found that approach very successful, and I have found other technical tools that help identify when turning points are about to arrive. There are times when Elliott is very clear and others when it is vague—much like any indicator. It is the price action that will prove the validity of the forecast.

Neal: Were you about to inform all your clients about the current bull market we are having? (The Dow was over 9000 during this interview.)

Nina: Exactly to the day.

Neal: Really?

Nina: Maybe to the hour. It's not difficult.

Neal: So is this market driven by low interest rates or by psychology?

Nina: It is purely driven by psychology. Markets are mechanisms to discount psychology.

Neal: Can you elaborate?

Nina: Markets are a means of discounting psychology. What that means is that despite all the wonderful economics and quantitative work, people buy markets because they believe they are going to go up. How they determine or justify their desire to buy is a whole different story. Likewise, they sell when they are afraid prices are going to go down. It's a matter of greed and fear. If you look at the psychological cycle in a move, the mood is always most negative at bottoms when those holding long positions can't stand the pain any longer. At tops, people are convinced that the rise will go on forever in a "new era." Smart money, or the really astute investors, are those able to withstand the conventional psychological pull and be there to buy when the crowd is liquidating and to sell to greedy longs who can't get enough. Even the most rational individuals seem to be overwhelmed by crowd psychology when it comes to markets.

Neal: Are we coming up to a new millennium; are we going to have what Herbert Hoover said, a "permanent prosperity"?

Nina: I think we're already there. I have to tell you, I do see a new millennium, but I don't think it's the euphoric millennium people talk about and would like to think it will be. I said you can use Elliott at a wide range of time horizons. That means that you can look back over a very long period of time, hundreds of years in fact, perhaps even farther back. And likewise, you can look far into the future.

Neal: Why is the millennium going to be different?

Nina: My view is that the millennium is going to be different in a way that people are not anticipating because the very long-term cycles are peaking.

Neal: The euphoria is like "happy days are here again." This is incredible, this is the biggest bull market in history. We are getting to a point in America that people don't have to work. They can just let the money work for them.

Nina: Yeah.

Neal: There are businesses that don't get the kind of return that the stock market is giving people.

Nina: Yeah, that's true.

Neal: Recently, I completed some seminars for a Florida software company. People are quitting work and letting the market work for them.

Nina: It sounds like a great idea, doesn't it? Likely, though, it's not a sustainable situation. That's the key. This bull market, this blow-off top we've seen over the last couple of years, is the last of a series of very long-term cycles. They are of varying lengths but are all finishing at roughly the same time. One very long cycle has been in progress since the 1800s. Now your average investor would have a hard time contemplating such a concept because memory is limited to what we know directly, and for many people, that's maybe 20 or so years. Even if you can incorporate what your parents might have told you about what it was like to live through the 1930s, it's not very immediate, and it doesn't strike any kind of emotional response with you. So trying to imagine something that began more than 100 years ago, 120 years ago, or 170 years ago is impossible.

Neal: Around the time Andrew Jackson was President.

Nina: That's right. The very long-term cycle that's ending is of that magnitude. The others are of shorter durations but are still so long that most of us don't have first-hand experience. All we basically know are markets of the last two or three decades. But those very slow cycles are being completed, and the implication is that conditions are going to change. I'm not forecasting an imminent collapse. What I am suggesting is that the correction that is about to begin is not only going to be correcting the bull market that began 15 years ago, but it will also be correcting the very long-term rally that started around 1840 or so. It will also be a sustained period, more than likely of erosion. Of course, there will be periods of market rallies and economic growth along the way, but the overriding trend will be for price deterioration. And once this "new era" begins, it's likely to stretch out over a very long period.

And that means that the euphoria that we're seeing now, the market highs that we are experiencing, could be the highs for a long time. We may be seeing the highs for our lifetime. The man in the street, the general public, would not have any concept of the cyclical change that I'm describing. I would be willing to bet that many people in government, maybe in central banks, don't adequately understand what people like me are talking about.

Neal: This kind of talk sounds very extreme.

Nina: I'll tell you why I feel it's important to be prepared to talk about the coming change. I believe there are times when our life circumstances are not as favorable as we might like. But that's the nature of life, ups and downs. Personally, I would prefer to know in advance when adversity was coming so I could prepare. I would rather be proactive, not reactive. As we know in the marketplace, there are opportunities regardless which way prices go. It is never uniformly negative. There are always bright spots. I would rather know when to be looking for these bright spots.

Neal: Let's say readers buy into this scenario. Maybe diversification is in order here. What do you think?

Nina: Yeah, I think the old story about diversification has enormous value. It probably has more value when the market is going down than when the market is going up. It means don't be heavily invested in one sector or one class of assets. Look for opportunities. There will be opportunities. When the broad stock market is under pressure, there will be other opportunities.

Neal: Like where? Real estate? Commodities?

Nina: I think real estate is one of the sectors that is going to be hit hard. It will be late; it will not come under pressure immediately. It's something to think about as you're planning your strategy. Those of us from the baby-boom generation are looking forward to retirement in the not-too-distant future. The demographics are a fact; the group behind us is smaller. Demographics mean that the property market will change, which makes it prudent to question whether holding a substantial portion of our portfolios in real estate is a wise thing.

Another area that is going to be very interesting and potentially rewarding in the years to come is the currency market. There's a lot going on there.

Neal: I know there are some people now who wish they had never heard of floating currencies. They wish they were on the gold standard.

Nina: The thing here is that there is a real major restructuring going on worldwide, not in the corporate sense, but in the sense of trade. Although we've heard tremendous amounts about Asian currencies and their respective stock markets, very few people in the United States talk about what's going on in Europe and the dynamics there. In the run-up for the creation of the Euro, the capital markets have been converging. And that convergence means that there will be fewer trading opportunities intra-Europe. It also means that once the Euro exists, there will be a new, viable alternative to the U.S. dollar as a reserve currency. And that implies potentially vast portfolio shifts around the world. Of course, all is based on the premise that the European Union, as a concept and an entity, will actually hang together. It's a glorious monetary experiment.

Neal: Do you think it will come unglued?

Nina: I think there is a risk that it will come unglued. I don't think it will completely shatter, though. Right now, the major markets, the European markets, the bond markets, and particularly the interest rate markets, are in the process of converging. The French, German, and Benelux markets are basically one, and they have been for some time. The countries historically at the margin, the high-yielding countries, are very close to converging as well. Anyone who has bought Italian bonds or Spanish *bonos* made a boatload of money because those interest rates converged. The governments of the high-yielding countries have done remarkable things to get themselves prepared to meet the criteria for inclusion in the monetary union, and the new currency, the Euro. However, it's yet to be seen whether or not those very stringent policies are going to be sustainable over time, and especially in the next cyclic downturn. Frankly, political resolve won't need to unravel. All the market needs to do is worry that the monetary union will unravel and we could see some massive swings. And the dollar is going to be the recipient of that volatility.

Neal: So the average person should start looking at other currencies than the dollar?

Nina: I would think so.

Neal: So "trading Chicago style" may get more involved in currencies?

Nina: I think it means we are going to be more international.

Neal: And maybe getting into currency funds?

Nina: That makes sense, particularly as the Euro develops.

Neal: So, you think we may see people trading gold or silver?

Nina: I expect precious metals' prices to begin to stir again. Gold in particular is completing a very long term correction, and the next rally should be strong, reflecting a breakout from a protracted basing period. Think of all the central banks that have divested their gold reserves in favor of paper currency reserves. If the U.S. dollar experiences high volatility, as I expect, gold may start to look attractive again. And what the central banks drove to 18-year lows, they potentially can drive to highs as well.

Neal: We're going through a time of deflation. How long do you think that's going to last?

Nina: I would argue that we're not going through a period of deflation. Some costs are declining, but prices in general continue to rise. Only the rate of change has slowed. There are few places in the world where price levels are falling generally. However, the very long-term cycles are probably shifting to the deflationary side, but we haven't faced those conditions yet.

Neal: In *Tricks of the Floor Trader*, I said we have inflation. When I repeat that notion in my fundamental analysis class, the students find it ridiculous, until they look at what they owe on their student loans.

Nina: I have the same problem. All you have to do is look at prices on day-to-day items to see that inflation is alive and well. There are some exceptions. Computers, telecommunications, and other technology-driven goods are cheaper. But housing, food, and service prices continue to rise. Look at the price of a car versus what it cost just 10 years ago. Although the rate of change has slowed down in recent years, the numbers are substantially higher than before. That slowing is not deflation. If you do historical research on inflation, you'll find very long-term cycles in inflation too. Historian David Hackett Fisher recently wrote a book, *The Great Wave*, about cycles in inflation. Beginning with medieval European price series data, he observed that since the 12th century, there have been four episodes of inflation, each running roughly between 90 and 120 years. During those periods, inflation starts from nothing and rises to a level which is unsustainable. At the peak of each cycle, some sort of crisis pricks the bubble. Centuries ago, the crises were violent. More recently, they have been political and especially economic. Either way, the events cleared away the previous structures, inflation ceased, and despite renewed economic and population growth, prices remained unchanged for decades. In fact, inflation typically is flat for nearly 100 years following a crisis period. The last noninflationary phase occurred during the Victorian era of the last century. After the Victorian period, the population growth and the resulting economic demands reach a critical point and the cycle begins again. This has happened four times since 1200.

We are at the end of one of those 100-year inflation cycles. My long-term cycle work suggests that the new millennium is probably not going to be a continuation of what we've seen in the last 20 or so years. Professor Hackett's inflation cycle suggests that real deflation is on the horizon, and there will probably be some kind of an event that triggers the approaching changes. What exactly is going to happen is impossible to forecast, but there is a high probability that conditions will be different, maybe much different from what we take for granted now. But for those who understand the message of cycles, there will be great opportunities.

Neal: Nina, thanks for sharing your thoughts.

Note: Nina Cooper can be e-mailed at: ngcooper@internetni. com.

There's No Such Thing as a Free Lunch

There is no such thing as a free lunch, but at one time you could get one.

The Chicago Board of Trade, founded in 1848 to promote and facilitate Chicago commerce, started with 82 members and no special interest in the grain business. The city's grain traders and merchants had no special interest in the Chicago Board of Trade either. In the early days, the Board attracted members with free lunches. Apparently, even that was not sufficient inducement. On four days in July 1851, only one member made an appearance, and no one showed up on four other days. Traders preferred to do business on the city's streets, amid piles of wheat and oats.

The Crimean War of the 1850s changed all that. The war boosted demand for American grain, which meant wheat shipments through Chicago rose in volume until it became easier for grain brokers to do their buying and selling in one central place.

With all the talk of the global economy, it is easy to forget that buyers of our grain came from Europe to do business here before the Civil War.

As its prominence in the grain trade grew, the Board adopted standards for the quality of commodities, with a bottom grade of "rejected." The grading system, first established in 1856, made it possible for traders to buy and sell quantities of a certain grade of wheat—not specific sacks of wheat, which was cumbersome at best. From there, it was a short step to buying and selling contracts for the delivery of grain in the future. The trading of futures, which took off after the Civil War, quickly outstripped trading of the real thing. By 1875, the *Tribune* reported the city's grain trade to be $200 million. The sale of grain futures was ten times that, $2 billion.

And over time, the current open-outcry system of floor trading evolved and took hold. However, those days are coming to an end as computer trading gains popularity.

The Chicago Board of Trade to this day remains the world's largest futures exchange, with markets not only in agricultural products but also in U.S. Treasury bond notes and other financial instruments, such as municipal bonds, and metals, among other products. And far from the days of the free lunch, traders now pay somewhat more for membership. In 1999, a full membership cost as much as $710,000.

Pit Stops

BACK-TESTING

This first letter is a testimonial to back testing.

> As a trader, I am convinced that back-tested mechanical
> trading systems can work. However, as a doctor I can tell
> you that one does develop a sixth sense of what's wrong
> and what to do about it even before all the tests are back.
> This puts you slightly ahead of the herd—be they bacteria
> or other traders, and a few minutes or a few hours can
> sometimes make the difference. In the scientific world, of
> course, one runs all the tests anyway because sometimes,
> you're just flat wrong. Still, my "doctor's intuition" is right
> about 80 percent of the time. Many mechanical trading
> systems cannot claim such a "percent profitable." I'm cer-
> tain there are professional traders out there who have the
> same sort of sensitivity about the markets, and they
> clearly have an advantage over more mechanical traders
> such as myself.
>
> Clint

This second letter is a response and rebuttal to the first letter.

> In the October issue of our favorite magazine (*Technical
> Analysis of Stocks and Commodities*), there is an interview
> with James O'Shaughnessy. This interview will be of in-
> terest to those who have a view on the validity of back-
> testing as a method for developing trading strategies. The
> most interesting point made by Mr. O'Shaughnessy is that
> back-tested models work best in all fields of human en-
> deavor, not just in trading. Such models, which he calls
> *quantitative/actuarial models,* consistently outperform
> nonback-tested models, which he calls *clinical/intuitive
> models.* This is as true for doctors attempting diagnoses as
> it is for handicappers picking horses at the track. It is as
> true for college administrators judging admissions candi-

dates as it is for parole boards judging parolees. It is as true for loan officers doing underwriting as it is for traders judging markets.

The key is to choose a model which performs well in back testing and then *stick to that model.*

Good trading,

Taken from omegalist@eskimo.com

You Don't Need to Back-Test; You Just Need Money

In the late 1960s, Ben Schwartz cornered the pork belly market. When I mentioned this to his daughter, she reminded me that her dad started the business with a $50 loan from his sister. By 1948, the business had become the largest independent beef-boning establishment in the country—not bad for a man who dropped out of high school. According to his daughter, Cathy Schwartz Cybak, "It's unfortunate you didn't meet my dad before he passed away in 1989. He was living proof that it takes guts, tenacity, and hard work to see an opportunity."

So how did Ben corner the market? It's because he owned a meat boning and packing plant located next door to the U.S. cold storage warehouse. So he could simply buy up the pork bellies and store them. And just when the word got out that there was a shortage of pork bellies, what do you think happened? Ben Schwartz sold his inventory. Since he owned the product, he was able to really bring home the bacon. To this day, I keep this story in mind. There are plenty of smart people without computers and software who understand the basic laws of supply and demand.

DICK QUITER

Indicators That Make Sense— at Least to Me

Dick is one of the most low-key brokers and advisors I have met. For more than 20 years, Dick's clients trading longevity in the market attest to his experience. When it comes to trading Chicago style, there are popular indicators used by traders and brokers. Here, Quiter talks about his favorite indicators.

Neal: Dick, let's talk about some of your favorite indicators. If you don't mind, I'm going to include some of the samples you are showing in this interview. So, what is your favorite indicator, Dick?

Dick: Well, I do not have one favorite indicator. And I wish to add, indicators are just that, indicators. Too much time is spent on indicators rather than on the fundamentals that drive the market. However, one indicator I do consider is divergence. This can be used to measure many concepts. Figure 3-1 demonstrates divergence between price and volume. While price was falling during the first two weeks of February, volume was increasing. This indicated a selloff, which finally ended at the end of the month, when prices once again began to climb.

Charts courtesy of Aspen Graphics. ©1999 Aspen Research Group Ltd.

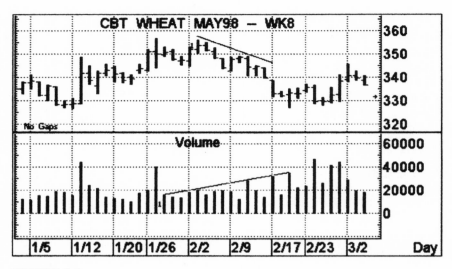

FIGURE 3-1.

Neal: Dick, you also have trend identifiers, right?

Dick: Yes, I like to use moving averages. Moving averages are used to identify the direction and strength of a trend. The steeper the moving average line, the stronger the trend.

Multiple moving averages can be used to identify entry and exit points. When the short-term moving average crosses the long-term moving average, it can be a sign that the general trend is changing. This is particularly useful when the crossing occurs in extremely high or extremely low territory, as seen in Figure 3-2.

The moving average convergence divergence (MACD) expands on the multiple moving average idea. The difference of two exponential moving averages with different numbers of periods is charted, and then an exponential moving average of that line is overlaid and used as a signal for entry and exit points, as explained above (see Figure 3-3). Here, the MACD line crossed over the signal line in low territory and quickly began to pull away from it. A rally ensued, the end of which was signaled by the MACD crossing below the signal line during the first week in March. I wish to caution that moving averages can also be dif-

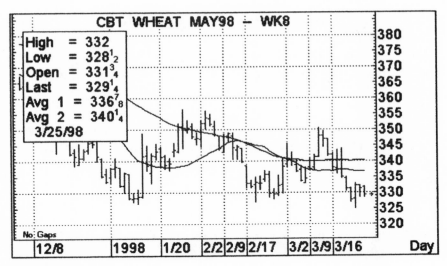

FIGURE 3-2.

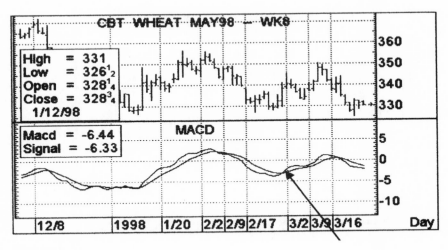

FIGURE 3-3.

ficult to trade in a sideways market. I like to think of moving averages as giving me a potential signal, a sort of setup if you will. I have seen too many trading systems based on moving averages and then have them optimized on a month-to-month basis.

Neal: I notice that you like to use different strengths of trend identifiers, like the directional movement index.

Dick: Yes.

Neal: Can you give me a definition of directional movement index?

Dick: Sure, Neal. Directional movement measures the strength of the trend, as seen in Figure 3-4.

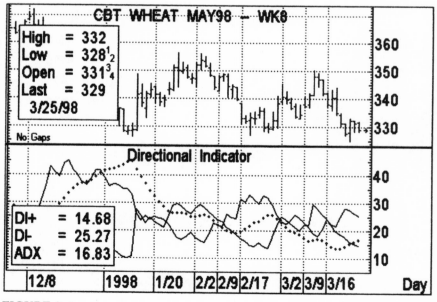

FIGURE 3-4.

Neal: I also notice, Dick, that another one of your favorite turning-point indicators is stochastics. How about a quick definition of that?

Dick: Stochastics is a turning-point indicator. The theory behind this indicator is fairly basic. Rising prices are usually accompanied by closes fairly near the highs of the range. Accordingly, prices that close near the middle may suggest a market that is not trending.

Neal: So what is % K?

Dick: Don't worry too much about that. Merely think of it as a stochastic value.

Neal: And what does % D value represent?

Dick: That's merely a moving average of the % K.

Neal: So % K will always move faster than % D?

Dick: Right, because % D is a moving average. Let me make it easy for you. In general, values below 30% mean oversold and values above 70% tend to mean overbought. The % K and % D lines have to *cross* above 70 or below 30.

Neal: So in a strongly trending market, a market can stay overbought as well as oversold?

Dick: I think Figure 3-5 helps illustrate the point.

Neal: What's another favorite indicator you like to use?

Dick: I also like a relative strength index (see Figure 3-6).

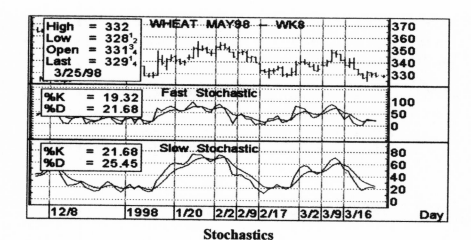

Stochastics

FIGURE 3-5. Stochastics.

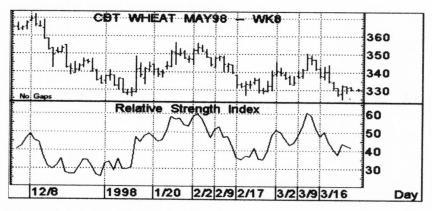

FIGURE 3-6. Relative strength index (RSI).

Neal: Is there anything you use for trend accelerators?

Dick: Just momentum, as shown in Figures 3-7 and accelera-tion, shown in 3-8, as pivot point indicators.

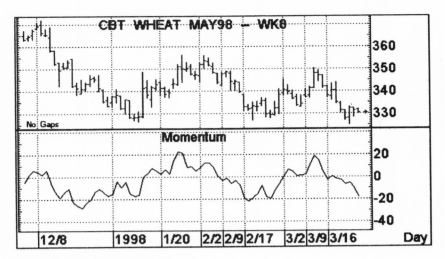

FIGURE 3-7.   Momentum.

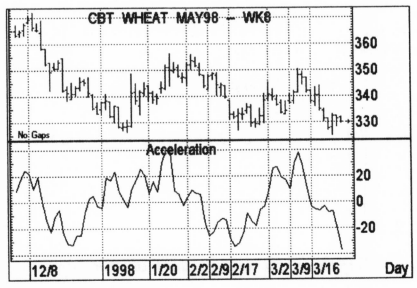

FIGURE 3-8.   Acceleration.

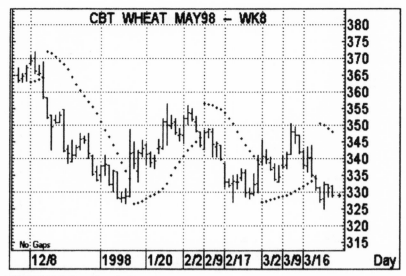

FIGURE 3-9.   Parabolic.

Neal: And I also notice that there's a parabolic. I think that's what you take when you have an upset stomach.

Dick: Ha! No, actually a parabolic is explained by Figure 3-9.

Neal: You also like to use Fibonacci retracement levels. Could you discuss that?

Dick: Well, that could be the subject of a whole book, but Figure 3-10 illustrates the basics.

Neal: Well Dick, thank you very much for this interview.

Dick: You're quite welcome, Neal. But remember, I use fundamentals to give me market direction and then use some of these technicals to fine-tune my entrance and exit strategy.

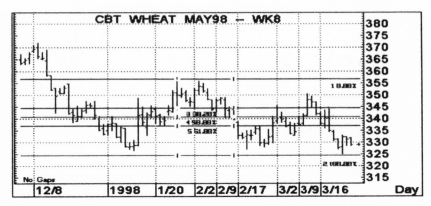

FIGURE 3-10.   Fibonacci retracement levels.

Neal: Thanks again, Dick. Basically, how many indicators do you think people need?

Dick: Not more than three, and be sure they are not measuring the same thing.

Neal: You mean like having lagging indicators and no leading indicators as with stochastics?

Dick: If I didn't know any better, I would swear you are definitely a high school graduate.

Neal: I really am, Dick, I really am.

Note: Dick Quiter may be reached at 1 (800) 234-8540, or at: dickquiter@aol.com.

Pit Stops

SURGICAL TRADING

The following letter was sent over the Internet to Mark Brown. It's priceless. His reply is invaluable for people hoping to make a quick buck trading futures. (Mark Brown has also done an interview in the book. See Chapter six.)

Dear Mr. Brown:

I happened to find your name and e-mail address in a newsgroup posting. I'm a 62-year-old surgeon, and I wonder if I might borrow a couple minutes of your time. I'm a complete novice to day-trading but I'm considering trying it. To date, I've bought and sold stocks and mutual funds on a very small time basis, holding most for months or years. I've always wanted to try day-trading, but I'm totally clueless as to the best way to learn day-trading.

Actually, what I'm planning to do is set up an exceedingly bright but completely green friend of mine with training, equipment, and data-feeds, and then let her go to town. She's a 36-year-old grad student (psychology/divinity) with an IQ over 188 and a Mensa card in her wallet . . . exceedingly bright but with zero experience also. There seem to be a few prominent players in the training market. I haven't the slightest idea if it makes sense to go to one of these courses and spend $1200 to $3000 for a few days (or as long as three weeks in the Dina course), or whether the same or more can be accomplished with books and/or home-study courses. One advantage of the Broadway course is that you can apparently watch day-traders at work during market hours. And, of course, I'll need books and data-feed services.

Can you make any recommendations as to how I should proceed? I'd be happy to pay you for your time.

Here is Mr. Brown's reply.

Give your money to a charity and you will feel much better than you will by having guys like me take it from you. I'm serious, this is a suckers' game, with very, very few pros taking home all the money. A high IQ is not going to help you. Let me turn the table. I want to be a doctor, could you recommend a good book for me to read? See, I'm planning on doing a few heart transplants out in my garage and retire soon. Please advise; if I must, I will spend the $3000 for a three-week seminar. I hate to spend that kind of money, but I will if I can have your assurance that I will learn it all.

Thank You,

Mark Brown

DON TRIVETTE

TRADING THE SPUS

Don Trivette represents a new kind of trader who is developing here in Chicago. Don trades in the pit and off the floor. He decided to try his skill at trading only after he had turned forty.

Neal: You're an S&P trader and you trade on and off the floor, correct?

Don: That's true. I trade for myself, and I will trade off the floor using the Globex terminals.

Neal: So, I imagine that the computer does not make you fearful the same way it concerns other traders.

Don: Not at all. In fact, I welcome the computer. You see, I believe that the market trades in trends, or cycles, if you prefer. A cycle includes both an up trend and a down trend to complete the "cycle," but I often use the two terms interchangeably. I think that the market trades in cycles (trends) of different lengths. Figure 4-1 is a hypothetical illustration of the relationship between two cycles of different lengths.

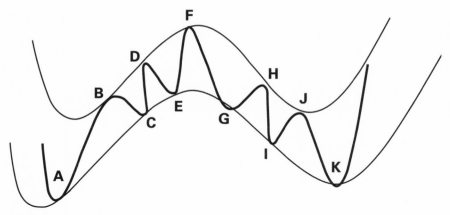

FIGURE 4-1.

Neal: Your diagram looks a little complicated.

Don: Well, at first it does, but look closer. The outer band represents a larger cycle, compared to a cycle of shorter length. This might be a cycle of an hourly inside the cycle of a daily chart. It also could be a cycle of a 10-minute chart within an hourly chart, or it might be a one-minute chart within a 10-minute chart.

A very aggressive day-trader will be looking at the one-minute chart, hoping to catch a very quick move of only a few minutes and only a point or two of profit. He needs to compare the cycles of the one-minute chart to the cycles of the 10-minute chart.

A less aggressive trader might be looking for only two or three trades a day. He would probably look at the 10-minute chart and compare it to an hourly chart.

An even longer-term trader might use the hourly compared to the daily to make two or three trades per week. A stock investor might use the daily compared to the weekly, or even the weekly to the monthly, to time stock trades.

The point is that you should know where you are on the larger cycle, even while you are trading a smaller cycle. You should be looking for buy signals at points *C* and *E*. You should be looking for sell signals at points *H* and *J*. You must be extremely careful if you try to buy at points *G* and *I*, or sell at points *B* and *D*. Points *A* and *F* are the turning points of the major cycles. These are the high-risk, high-reward trades. Some traders always try to pick the turning points. Some traders prefer less risky trades.

Please note that this is a hypothetical illustration. There can be several up waves or several down-waves in a full major cycle. I have only illustrated five little cycles within the larger cycle. There could be more. There probably will not be fewer.

Also, there may be more up-waves than down waves, or vice versa. This would probably be because of the effect of the next larger cycle. The whole point is to trade in sync with the larger cycle. If you would like to know more about cycles, I suggest that you study Elliott Wave theory. I am not a pure Elliott Wave Theorist, but I do think that it might be helpful.

Neal: In terms of real-world trading, how do you trade?

Don: Throughout the day; I am constantly drawing trendlines. Usually, I also draw a parallel line through a significant point to form a channel. A channel gives a very good visual picture of the short-term trend. To draw the channel shown in Figure 4-2, all that was needed were points *A*, *B*, and *C*.

If the market breaks a channel slightly but comes back within it, I will modify the lines. I am constantly correcting my trendlines to give as accurate a picture of the market as possible.

I am also constantly evaluating whether I expect the market to trade within this channel, or if I anticipate a breakout. I use other factors, such as stochastics, to help in evaluating this possibility.

I have just received an e-mail from a friend who sold short December soybean meal early last week. He put a $3.00 stop on his trade. Of course, he got stopped out. Of course, December meal is now lower. (I am not making fun of my friend. I am just venting my frustration at using stops. When I use a stop, the market always hits me and then reverses. When I don't use a stop, it is amazing how far the market goes against me!)

He asked me to comment. Here are some thoughts.

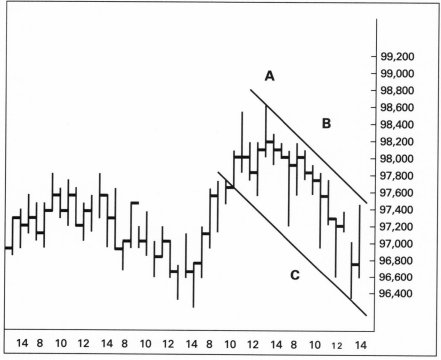

FIGURE 4-2.

Neal: Sure, go ahead. I think other traders would be interested.

Don: First of all, I don't have the option prices as of when he made the trades, so I am going to imagine that he is considering shorting December meal at Friday's closing price (September 4). Therefore, I can look at some options as a possible choice.

December meal is $131.80. In lieu of futures, maybe buy a deep in-the-money put. The December 140 put is trading for $10.60. It is $8.20 in the money. If meal goes down, he will make $2.40 less than shorting the futures. (This is the time-value value above the amount in the money.)

What he has is a position that has limited risk. He does not have to initiate a stop. This gives him a better chance of having the market work for him. Of course, this is not exactly fair, since the option cost $10.60, while he only risks $3.

The point of all this discussion is that buying an in-the-money option is often better than using futures. You probably will not have to pay too much above intrinsic value. You can avoid using a stop. Just think of all the trades you have made where you got stopped out and then the market went in your favor.

The following is a hypothetical illustration:

October gold closed today (September 9) at $285.10. October 285 gold puts closed at $1.50.

Strategy:

Buy five October gold futures, and buy ten October 285 gold puts. (For simplification in the math, let's pretend that we have bought the five futures for $285.00.) The ten puts cost $15.00 each, for a total of $150. Except for commissions, this is the maximum risk on this strategy.

Scenario 1: October gold goes up.

   At 286, sell one contract. Profit on this contract is $1.00
   At 287, sell one contract. Profit on this contract is $2.00
   At 288, sell one contract. Profit on this contract is $3.00
   At 289, sell one contract. Profit on this contract is $4.00
   At 290, sell one contract. Profit on this contract is $5.00

                                            Total received $15.00

Scenario 2: Gold goes down.

   At 284, buy one contract. Profit on this contract is $1.00
   At 283, buy one contract. Profit on this contract is $2.00
   At 282, buy one contract. Profit on this contract is $3.00
   At 281, buy one contract. Profit on this contract is $4.00
   At 280, buy one contract. Profit on this contract is $5.00

                                            Total received $15.00

If the market goes lower, the profit on these contracts is calculated from a sell price of 285, the strike price of the put options.

In both of these cases, you make enough money back to pay for the put options. But what if gold doesn't go up to 290 or down to 280? Here is scenario 3:

If gold goes up to 286, sell one contract. If it goes back to 285, buy it back for a $1.00 gain. If gold goes back up to 286, sell one contract. If it goes up to 287, sell another contract. If it drops back to 286, buy back the contract that was sold at 287 for a profit of $1.00 on this trade. If it falls to 285, buy back the contract sold at 286 for a $1.00 profit on this trade. If gold drops to 284, buy a contract. If it rallies back to 285, sell it for a $1.00 profit.

Each time gold rallies $1.00, sell a contract until you run out of contracts. Each time gold drops $1.00, buy a contract until you own ten contracts. Each time you get one of these swings, you make $1.00. If you get fifteen swings, you have the cost of the puts back.

The ideal situation is for gold to run up and down several times and let you get a lot of these swing trades put in your pocket. Then, hopefully, it will run straight up or straight down and let you collect the fifteen points from either scenario 1 or scenario 2.

Neal: I understand you offer an Internet course that's free and easier to grasp than what you just said.

Don: Yes, I started doing it so people could bite off morsels of information.

Neal: You know, volatility is an important consideration in trading.

Don: True.

Neal: So give me an example of how you explain volatility over the Internet.

Don: You mean you want a sample Internet chapter?

Neal: Yes, why not . . . this book needs a "freebie."

Don: I call this Intermediate Commodity Options #25.

Volatility is a very difficult factor to explain, but it should not be that difficult to understand. An option that is out of the money has a hope that the futures price will move there before the time runs out. This hope could be based on many factors. One factor would be how the futures have been moving lately—historical volatility of the futures. If the futures are 1150, but they were over 1240 last week, then it would not be unreasonable to think the market might go back above 1240 in the next four weeks. Or, if the futures are 1150 now, but they were 1050 last week, then it might not be unreasonable to expect the market to rally another 100 points in the next four weeks. In this case, you would expect the 1240 call to have a significant value.

There is a formula to calculate historical volatility. I am not going to give you the formula here. Suffice it to say that you would need a computer to calculate historical volatility. What is done is to take a certain number of days (usually 20), calculate the range of the futures for all of the days—and also the range as a whole—and crunch these numbers into an index.

If the futures have not had such wild price action, the option values would certainly be less. But perhaps there is a government report due that usually causes the market to move dramatically. The option traders will want a higher premium to compensate for the risk of being short the option during the report. This extra value above the actual volatility might be called "anticipatory volatility."

There is another way that professional traders measure volatility, called "implied volatility." This is also a very complicated formula. You will need a computer to calculate it. Generally, the way it is calculated is to take the options value, compare it to the number of days remaining in the life of the contract and the amount that it is in or out of the money, and then calculate the formula backwards to see what volatility in the futures would be necessary to "imply" the actual premium.

Let me explain volatility in simple language. Volatility affects an option's value in the same way as time does. More volatility means a higher option value. More time means a higher value. Less volatility means a lower option value. Less time means a lower option value. Time and volatility are closely related.

If you have lots of time but no volatility, you will have a low option premium. If you have high volatility but no time left, you again have a low option premium. You need both time and volatility to have a high option premium.

How does volatility affect vertical call spreads that we discussed? Here are the prices of the call options on the December S&P futures as of the close on November 18, 1998:

Option Month	Price	Difference
Dec 1240	@ the call 1.10	
		0.80 > difference in price (amount paid by buyer)
Dec 1230	@ the call 1.90	
Dec 1210	@ the call 4.80	
		2.20 > difference in price (amount paid by buyer)
Dec 1200	@ the call 7.00	

These two spreads are out of the money. Less volatility will decrease the value of each option and also the value of each spread. If we suddenly had extremely low volatility, these options as well as the spreads would suddenly approach zero.

Now look at the next two examples:

OPTION MONTH	PRICE	DIFFERNCEE
Dec 1110	@ the call 56.10	
		7.90 > difference in price (amount paid by buyer)
Dec 1100	@ the call 64.00	
Dec 1030	@ the call 125.40	
		9.30 > difference in price (amount paid by buyer)
Dec 1020	@ the call 134.70	

All of these options are in the money. If the volatility suddenly dropped, all of these options would lose value, approaching their intrinsic value. But since the spreads are in the money, the actual spread values would go up, approaching 10.00. This is exactly the same effect as a drop in time.

When a vertical spread is in the money, a drop in volatility benefits the spread's value.

Neal: This vertical spread contract is really advanced options.

Don: Yes, but if you trade Chicago style, as I do, you must understand options, because you can gauge how volatile the futures will be.

Neal: Thanks for the lesson.

Don: That will cost you lunch.

Neal: Taco Bell, here we come.

Pit Stops

Types of Traders

There are many types of traders. An awareness of the variety allows you to avoid some of the pitfalls.

The Disciplined Trader. This is the ideal type of trader. You take losses and profits with ease. You focus on your system and follow it with discipline. Trading is usually a relaxed activity. You appreciate that a loss does not make you a loser.

The Doubter. You find it difficult to execute at signals. You doubt your own abilities. You need to develop self-confidence. Perhaps you should paper-trade.

The Blamer. All losses are someone else's fault. You blame bad fills, your broker for picking the phone up too slowly, your system for not being perfect. You need to regain your objectivity and self-responsibility.

The Victim. You blame yourself. You feel the market is out to get you. You start becoming superstitious in your trading.

The Optimist. You start thinking, "It's only money, I'll make it back later." You think all losses will bounce back to a profit or that you will start trading properly tomorrow.

The Gambler. You are in for the thrill. Money is a side issue. Risk and reward analysis hardly figure in your trades. You want to be a player, to have the buzz and excitement.

The Timid Trader. You enter a trade but panic at the sight of a profit and take it far too soon. Fear rules your trading.

GRANT D. NOBLE

CHICAGO IS NOT NEW YORK. GET IT?

Grant Noble and I have known each other since we appeared on a television show here in Chicago. He is the author of the book *The Trader's Edge*.

Neal: How would you compare Chicago-style trading with other cities?

Grant: Chicago is definitely friendlier than most other money centers. For example, I recently sent out a report claiming that technicians are media stars now and are getting paid more than their fundamentalist counterparts. One guy from New York called me and said this wasn't true because high-tech analysts get paid more than technicians on Wall Street. I asked him whether the average steel, auto, retail, etc., analyst you see on TV was getting paid more than the "TV star" technician. My point is that the average fundamental analyst you see on TV is getting paid less than the average technician you see on TV. But many people are so interested in putting you down that they will look for the faintest error on your part, no matter how stupid it makes them look. The rest of the world seems to have also given up trying to figure out how to trade the markets. They either concentrate on what they can foist on the public (the latest investment fad), or they concentrate on getting insider information ("whisper numbers" on corporate earnings, what the Fed is likely to do, "the Treasury Secretary told me yesterday," etc.), which is only useful for a very limited time frame in very specific markets.

Neal: Well, we all are not a bunch of saints here either, are we?

Grant: Of course, we also have plenty of con artists in Chicago peddling the latest investment fads. But maybe it is due to the fact that there isn't an insider pipeline to whether this summer is going to be dry or wet. I don't see a big scramble for insider information in Chicago. Chicago concentrates on what works versus what sells. And what works is sophisticated technical analysis, not the tripe usually peddled as "technical analysis." The massive commodity bull of 1973–1974 created an awe of technical analysis among futures traders. While "fundamentalists" stood and watched "impossible moves," technicians like Gene Cashman and Richard Dennis became megamillionaires. Before that, technicians were crazies who met in back rooms and discussed their charts in low voices lest anyone hear them. Now they became gods who could do no wrong. The track record of most "technicians" in futures has been lousy since then, but this did give some of the smarter traders a head start in studying what actually works. The brighter minds of the futures industry are now rapidly moving away from another computerized permutation of the "sacred six" (open, high, low, close, volume, and open interest).

Neal: So how do you see the stock and bond side of the business?

Grant: In my opinion, the stock and bond industries have reached the same position that futures were in 20 years ago. An unprecedented bull market has shattered every "fundamental" rule in the stock market. Traditional indicators have been left in the dust as the stock market soared (vs. the GDP) to a valuation 50% greater than in 1929. (That is one comparison that can't be explained away by "new paradigm" excuses!) Stock technicians have so vanquished stock fundamentalists that news (Clinton's scandals, Buffett's silver buying, Yeltsin's threats against the U.S. in the Iraq crisis) and astronomical valuations that would have sent stocks plunging in the past are now greeted with a yawn and the words, "The momentum is up." Twenty years ago, in the glory days of technical analysis in futures, I tried to study everything I could about technical analysis. I read the "old masters," like Elliott, Gann, Edwards and McGee, Wykoff, Andrews, and others in the original, not relying on the popularizers. After long and painful periods of study and attempts to use the methods I learned, I concluded the spectacular results of "technicians" during the 1973 to 1980 period were flukes based on the power of trend-following. But even trend-following was losing its punch as more and more "breakouts" failed, because they were simply the result of mindless buying and/or selling by the "technicians," who now dominate futures.

Neal: I remember the days when you avoided technical analysis.

Grant: For a long time, I was so disgusted at traditional technical analysis I hardly looked at a chart. I spent my time on cycles, public sentiment, and using traditional technical methods on nonprice data. Slowly but surely, I have come to realize the best form of technical analysis brings price back to its rightful place alongside time and sentiment in predicting long-term trends. But we must realize three things:

1. Because of inflationary bias, bear market analysis has not gotten the attention it deserves. But after inflation, there have been many "stealth" bear markets, like stocks from 1968 to 1982. Since bear markets unfold quite differently from bull markets, no wonder many periods of trading are

completely baffling to the practitioners of traditional technical analysis. We have to radically adjust our indicators to trade bear markets effectively.

2. Markets where most participants are highly leveraged trade differently than markets where leverage is muted.

3. Prices must be adjusted to reflect today's economic reality (i.e., they must be currency- and inflation-adjusted).

Neal: So you did an almost 360-degree turnaround of opinion.

Grant: I have slightly modified what I preached in my book. In the old days, I would have said sentiment is the most important indicator and that the best indicator of sentiment is media. Today, I have far more confidence in inflation and currency-adjusted charts which you can use on markets not covered by the media and analyze before the latest edition of *The Wall Street Journal* comes out.

Neal: Okay, Grant, what is your favorite technique now?

Grant: My favorite technique in the final critical factor in market analysis (time) is something else I have discovered since my book came out. I call it "anniversary days." For example, the Dow topped in the spring of 1997, on March 10—exactly 60 years after its 1937 top. But unlike Gann, who used a few preset long-term cycles to determine anniversary days, I try to use every cycle that has been proven to have validity in a certain commodity, index, etc., to determine all the anniversary days for the year.

Neal: So it is a matter of combining many techniques?

Grant: In the end, nothing can take the place of a trader analyzing and combining all the data into his own winning pattern. Woody Hayes said three things can happen when you pass the football and two of them are bad. In systems, there are three things that can happen, and two of those are bad. You can have a bad system (or a system "optimized" to work in only one market, like stocks, or one environment, like the bull market). You can have a good system but not trust it enough to follow every signal. To get a system you can trust and use, you must know its parameters and strengths or weaknesses. In other words, you are never going to purchase a "system" whose results year in and year out are better than the average trend-following system. So you may as well design your own and stop frustrating yourself.

Neal: Well, the people advertising trading systems won't like to hear this, and neither will people promoting back-testing software packages.

Grant: The best advice is to read everything you can and practice before you trade real money. It's amazing how people will spend years of study and thousands of dollars to become a lawyer or a doctor, but somehow they think they can enter the high income profession of futures trader without doing a bit or preparation. Again and again, I have seen public traders lose tens of thousands of dollars and be none the wiser after all their time and money. They should have put that lost $10,000 into buying every futures book they could find. All that time watching prices could have been poured into a self-directed "college course" learning about the market. Nothing is going to work until you have confidence it is going to work, and that takes time.

Neal: So buying a piece of software won't cut it.

Grant: Right.

Neal: Will Chicago style open outcry disappear?

Grant: No, but it's obvious U.S. futures exchanges will go to the solution (10 years too late) the CBOE came to about a decade ago. The CBOE uses computer matches for their low-volume products, while their flagship products like the OEX use computer matches for "odd lot" (under 10 contracts) trades instead of going to the floor. The new Emini S&P 500 contract is certainly the wave of the future in futures. But I don't think futures exchanges outside the U.S., no matter how much they cut costs through computerized trading, are going to take away U.S.-dominated markets like grains, meats, and U.S. securities from U.S. exchanges. Of course, overseas exchanges will continue to nip at the heels of the U.S. exchanges and force cost-cutting and changes. This is why we are getting more electronic trading and talks about common clearing between hated rivals like the CME and CBOT. But in the end, chauvinism and the need of the locals to preserve open outcry will prevail. The best example of this is how New York took over gold futures trading. We had a perfectly good market here in Chicago, and there was no cost savings in relocating to expensive New York, but the hometown chauvinism of the New York security firms and cash gold brokers forced trading away from Chicago to New York. There will simply be too much institutional pressure in the U.S. for overseas competition to totally succeed, and there will be too much internal pressure from exchange members for the U.S. exchanges to totally stop open outcry.

Neal: Do we really need futures exchanges, or will big banks take over the clearing functions?

Grant: Tell me, if you were a big stock house like Goldman Sachs, where would you like to do more of your trading, on an exchange floor where you have voting clout or with a big bank that may own one of your rivals like Salomon Brothers? Even in Japan, a society dominated by a handful of banks, futures trading has flourished. In this world you shouldn't say never, but the odds favor the continuation of open outcry at futures exchanges for the foreseeable future.

Neal: Nina Cooper thinks that the future beyond the year 2000 is not as optimistic as it was in the recent past. Do you agree?

Grant: Yes, wholeheartedly. Baby boomers like myself have seen nothing but a perpetual bull stock market since 1974. But there are three reasons to expect a vast decline in U.S. stocks and the U.S. economy over the next decade. The first reason is demographic. The bottoms of stock markets this century (as in 1982) have always been at the bottom of the "saver/spender ratio," which measures the number of "spenders" (people between 24 and 34 who have to borrow for new houses and babies) and "savers" (people from 40 to 49 who reach their peak earnings and savings rate before retirement, illness, and college costs reach them). In the past stocks have peaked at the same time the five-year rate of change of this ratio has peaked or at the actual peak of this ratio. The peak in the five-year rate of change of the saver/spender ratio came last spring, and the peak of the actual ratio will come in 2002. While some people are using the later date to justify stock purchases, it should be noted that in the market that most resembles our own (1929), it peaked at the peak of the five-year rate of change in the saver/spender, not the demographic top in 1935. That brings me to the second reason for a stock and overall economic decline. The stock market is so overvalued, it would have to fall 70 percent just to get back to historic norms in terms of dividend yields, price to book, price to peak earnings, the size of the stock market compared to our economy, the 100-year trendline in total returns in the Dow, and so on. During this incredible bull market, we have had a "wealth effect" that has sustained our economy as flush investors and desperate foreigners looking for a good economy have pumped money into our consumer sectors. But once stocks begin to sell off, as they have in Asia, we will have a reverse wealth effect that will cause our economy to collapse like the Asian economies did, with a credit collapse and panic foreign selling. By the year 2000, the saver/spender ratio will reach a bottom in Japan, while ours won't reach a bottom for more than a decade afterward. After 1999, it will make more sense demographically to invest in Japan than here.

The third reason is political and socioeconomic. My generation (the baby boomers) have been hopelessly brainwashed by liberal educrats to expect the government to solve their problems. Like Japan and Europe in the 1990s, any economic decline will be met with cries for more federal intervention, not tax cuts and privatization. If we can't cut taxes with the biggest Federal surpluses in history, and if we can't privatize Social Security despite the biggest bull stock market of all time, what makes anyone think that we are going to do anything different when times get tough? All this additional government (just like the New Deal did in the 1930s) will cause us to lag behind the rest of the world in recovering from the next depression. Japan and Europe have already tried to government-spend their way out of their messes. Now they are moving slowly but surely to more free market solutions out of sheer desperation. I think the Republicans will gain total power in 2000, just in time to preside over a severe economic downturn that will cause them either to flee their conservative rhetoric and totally turn to liberal solutions or to lose power in the 2002 elections. I expect the U.S. in the first decade of the 21st century to be like Japan in the 1990s, an economic basket case that doesn't have a clue how to get out of depression.

Note: Grant Noble can be reached at: gnoble@safeplace.net; fax: (847) 234-3520.

WHAT TRADING CAN AND CANNOT BUY

A bed but not sleep
Books but not brains
Food but not appetite
Finery but not beauty
A house but not a home
Medicine but not health
Luxuries but not culture
Amusements but not happiness
Companions but not friends
Flattery but not respect
Passion but not compassion
Flash but not class

MARK BROWN

WHY THE BAD BOYS OF COMMODITIES TRADE SYSTEMS FROM THE HIP

The name Mark Brown makes some people run the other way. He is candid, direct, and frank, quite a change from the "spin control" propaganda usually dished out to traders. Based in Dallas, Mark is a money manager and system trader.

Neal: What markets do you trade?

Mark: German bonds, Italian bonds, Long Gilt overseas 30-year bonds, S&P 500, Japanese yen, ten-year notes, and the Dow Jones Industrial Average.

Neal: You are a system trader? Correct?

Mark: Yes, completely, no seat of the pants at all, although I did in the past. I'm not a textbook trader, and knowing it makes me a better trader. I can't control my emotions like some of the great traders can. I am like a gunslinger. When I get in trouble, I may win the fight. I may get wounded and win the fight. I may get wounded, win the fight, and die later from the wound. But I'm going to win the fight, if it kills me. So if I can win the fight when I get in trouble, why can't I just either stay in trouble or figure out how to define what it is that I do to get out of trouble and just apply that all the time. So I took the time to painstakingly write down every detail of what I do. Then when I thought I had it all defined, I discovered there is more. So I went back and wrote the code. I learned by working for some very big successful traders. They would want me to program their years of intuitive trading style into a mechanical system. It can be done, but I need all the facts on paper. If they can't write it down, even to the smallest detail, then how can I read their minds? They have done so many things through the years that it becomes second nature to them, and they forget that they do it. If a person says that you can't program their intuitive trading style into a system, then they just don't know what their system is. Even if the rules change or are adaptive, that can be programmed also. Not many programmers will take the time to do code this way, and they cheap-shot it. I only did work for real-life successful traders. I didn't waste my time if they weren't for real. Why reinvent the wheel? Let's just put some rubber on it and make it better. Let's have the computer pick apart the intuitive trader's style and make it better. I must crutch by using a computer to trade. What I was afraid would get me labeled as a not-so-great trader has in fact made me a great trader. I don't have nerves of steel, but I have an instinct for honesty in testing, reality in trading, and I am a perfectionist at building trading systems. I would never go back to intuitive trading. I want to manage too much money, and the computer can trade better than I can any day.

Neal: Are you going to keep your current system?

Mark: I am. I am going to scientific software that is proprietary and Linux as an operating system. I use HP UNIX for the Ned Davis software now and a Sun Sparc 4 Unix. They don't *ever* crash.

Neal: Do you train traders?

Mark: I train everybody I come in contact with, but few (none) will listen. It is a lonely world in trading.

Neal: How do you or I build a system without knowing how it works?

Mark: Great! I have you where I want you! How did you drive a car at first, when you had not yet mastered constructing one with your own hands? How did you ride in a car for the first time without knowing yourself how to drive? How did you fly in an airplane for the first time, not having constructed it yourself? How do you enjoy looking out of a glass window not knowing fully the manufacturing process? How do you wipe your butt with toilet paper, not having made it with your own hands? How do you use a computer, not having made all the hardware with your own hands? On and on and on I could go!

Don't you get it? You can't build a system and don't have a system so a system can't exist for you? Wrong. You don't want a system, you want control. I don't know why some things work that I use, but I use them. I have faith that after years of seeing systems kick my butt that I can do no better on my own with discretion. You want to make it. You want to build it. You want what you want, but what matters to me is the final results. I don't care what process or method or amount of control I have along the way. You are different. I bet if you took a test, you would find that you would be suited for law enforcement. There is nothing wrong with that, but recognize what your end goals are and get there.

When it comes to systems and software programming and mathematics, I concede that I know little to nothing about them. Humble is above where I stand regarding these. Stupid is more like my self-assessment of those capabilities.

I am no smarter than you in these areas, but I am resourceful and I don't give up.

Neal: Thanks Mark.

Note: You can contact Mark Brown at: markbrown@mark brown.com. You can visit his Web site at: www.markbrown. com.

Pit Stops

THE FAILURES OF BACK-TESTING

This is a letter sent to Mark Brown.

Dear Mark,

First let me thank you for all your posts. I'm one who really appreciates all you do and try to do. I'm one of those sad naive cases who fell victim to dishonest system vendors. I bought Wisdom of the Ages for $10,000 last September. My business failed and after day-trading S&P 500 on paper, using the trial version, I made between $3000 and $11,000 per day. Even though the indicators had to be watched manually and required my novice interpretation, I was naively impressed, took the plunge and handed over 10 grand. When I got back from Chicago and started trading real-time with real money, I noticed that the 50-second fill-time getting in and again getting out of a trade, coupled with the bad fills and slippage (I estimate to be 40 cents) was something that was cleverly misrepresented by both the system vendor and the broker he set me up with. I lost $26,000—and stopped trading. I've been collecting (free downloads) systems and indicators since then and have them coming out the wazoo.

My back-testing has found nothing that works on day-trading. The closest I came was a simple pivot point system I wrote myself. It lost $8000 during December, and made about $20,000 until March 11th, using 1 contract paper trades with $175.00 slippage and commissions. As I said, I have tons of systems and indicators, mostly due to your generosity. Any chance you could make some suggestions of which ones are worthwhile testing?

Thanks.

MIKE CIRKS

Options Chicago Style

M ike has one of the best Web sites for options traders. Many of the traders who trade options Chicago style seek out his Web page.

Neal: Mike, give the reader a little background.

Mike: Well, I will try. I have a B.A. in political science from the University of Chicago. After school, I worked on the bond floor of the CBOT for First Options. After clerking on the floor, I moved to the proprietary trading department and became a trading systems developer. First Options was bought by Continental Bank, and I got to see the bank side of the business. When the proprietary group was disbanded, I did freelance programming, which evolved into an options risk analysis program. Soon after, I joined Phoenix Trading, where I wrote and maintained the trading system as well as trading in the Eurodollar options pit full time. After an extremely slow year of Euro trading, I left to form PM Publishing, which has been developing software for options traders all over the world since 1991. Currently, our business is evenly split between the CME, CBOT, New York exchanges, and overseas. Most of our customers are brokerage desks, pit traders and brokers, bank trading floors, and large hedge funds. Our program, the Professional Options Package, stands out because it is written from the perspective of full-time options traders.

Neal: Have options had a big impact on the way people trade?

Mike: Well, I believe there are four areas that I would like to review.

1. Since options pricing theory is based on principles from thermodynamics, options have brought physicists to the pits. Therefore, it is not based as much on who you know as what you know.

2. Options markets have made it safer for futures traders to put on bigger positions. Therefore, the futures business owes much to the options side. As the volume and liquidity have increased, the pits have become more competitive.

3. The toughness of a competitive option pit, such as the bond and Euro pits, is equal to the physical strains of the futures pits. The same tactics of turning markets and intimidating brokers work in the options pit. Instead of turning the direction of the futures price, they turn the direction of the straddle price. They can bid up or sell down volatility.

4. Just as with futures, Chicago options traders lead the world. They routinely use the full spectrum of trading strategies and have a wide variety of opinions and technology that they employ. The markets are generally tight and efficient. Pit traders hate this since they trade the bid/ask spread, but it is great for the retail public, who get better fills.

Mike Cirks can be contacted at: mike@pmpublishing.com.

Pit Stops

THE PROS AND CONS OF BEING A PIT TRADER

There are advantages and disadvantages to being a pit trader.

Advantages	Disadvantages
Execute your own trades.	Say goodbye to regular paychecks.
Substantial commission-reduction for members.	Say goodbye to corporate perks and benefits.
Up close and personal with the economy.	No FDIC to bail you out on a bad day.
You and *only* you control your fortunes; your abilities determine your success, not someone else's! You are the boss.	Little or no sympathy on a bad day.
You know where you stand at the end of each day.	Losses are immediate, like gains.
You can't beat the excitement.	Out trades or mistakes can be costly.
The length of lunch hours and vacations is determined by you; no punching a time clock.	Standing, sore throats, physical punishment.

THE PHANTOM

Why System Traders Blow Up and Out of the Market

There is an old saying that Vegas is one town that never sleeps. I'm sure this applies to the Phantom. Meeting the Phantom in Las Vegas drove home the fact that between speculation and gambling, there is a very thin line.

Neal: I think people would appreciate knowing more about your background.

Phantom: I was an accountant for 20 years in Chicago, and I currently reside in Las Vegas. I have undergraduate degrees in finance and accounting and an MBA. I started trading about eight years ago. Like most traders, I did not do well when I started. Fortunately, I had enough sense to stop trading and realized that without adopting a professional, businesslike approach to speculation, I would have very little chance achieving long-term success. I quickly realized that a disciplined money management methodology was absolutely essential for profitable trading. I eventually was able to apply the business knowledge I acquired as an accountant and applied it to the trading arena. The end result was money management software I named Macho Man, which is the only practical software providing the trader with the capability of managing trading similar to how you would a successful business. I also modified the software for horse and sports bettors as well as blackjack players, and those versions are used by most professional bettors here in Las Vegas. I discovered a statistical anomaly in the six-deck shoe game of blackjack, so in addition to trading, I play a lot of blackjack as well as sports betting. Having sophisticated money management software is also an absolute prerequisite for those activities.

Neal: You are generally known as not being a big fan of hypothetical trading or back-testing. Trading Chicago style means real trading, not "paper trading."

Phantom: Unfortunately, we cannot decide hypothetically to go ahead and make our mortgage and automobile payments and hypothetically send our children through college, so I don't see the hypothetical advantage of back-testing a system. It really gives one a false sense of confidence.

Neal: Well, there are certain advantages traders should know about.

Phantom: Well, there is an advantage known as *statistical advantage*. This advantage occurs when the payoff in a game is structured to favor one of the players. For instance, in roulette, a casino will pay you 35 to 1 if you hit a number rather than the true payoff of 38 to 1. In this case, one of the players has obtained an advantage by altering, or manipulating, the true payoff for a wagering event. It is impossible for any trader to achieve a manipulated statistical advantage because no one can state categorically that a profitable trader will continue to be a profitable trader 5 or 10 years from now. There are many stories of traders making millions of dollars only to lose it all at some later date. Likewise, traders who were unprofitable have suddenly become profitable only to become overconfident and arrogant and then return to unprofitability. In essence, future profitability or unprofitability is unpredictable based on past performance. On the other hand, the manipulated statistical advantage enjoyed by casinos will consistently produce profits forever, provided that limits are set on how high a bet can be made so that one bet will not bankrupt the house. That's the reason why every game in Las Vegas has an upper limit on how much you can wager on any one bet. There will be short-run fluctuations in profitability based on normal, 2 or 3 standard deviations from the mean, but in the long run, the casino will get all the money. That is why casinos are open 24 hours a day, 7 days a week—to get into the long run and handle as many bets as possible. That is how you play a game where you have the edge, get into the long run by taking as many bets as possible and never risk more than a small percentage of capital on any one bet.

Neal: What do you think of system traders?

Phantom: As I mentioned previously, I think trading a mechanical system which has been back-tested provides certain psychological benefits inasmuch as the trader has some idea of how the system performed in the past, such as worst drawdown, worst consecutive series of unprofitable trades, percentage of profitable trades, etc. Some individuals require this type of psychological crutch, sort of like wanting to know how far they will fall before they land if they jump into a black hole. The downside of following a mechanical system is that you must take every trade and not second-guess the system. This becomes very difficult to do. When you have those three or four losers in a row, you start to hesitate pulling the trigger when the next trading signal presents itself. Referring back to my previous analogy, trading a mechanical system for me is like fighting a war by following a military textbook that tells you how to position your troops, when to attack, and so forth. A battlefield is dynamic and fluid, just like the market. You must have the capacity to react quickly and decisively and improvise if need be. Following a prescripted battle plan limits your flexibility and capacity to improvise just like trading a mechanical system. Personally, I did not evolve into a more profitable trader by having a computer massage a bunch of numbers and make trading decisions for me. That is why I keep large, hand-drawn charts, so I can get the feel of the market and maintain sufficient flexibility to react to the current price structure. Keeping my own charts provides me with what fighter pilots call situational awareness, being cognizant of what is occurring all around you so you can plan and rapidly execute the appropriate offensive or defensive maneuver. The same comparison applies to playing blackjack. What is currently happening on the table, and do I exploit a perceived weakness and attack or is it time to pull back and retreat? In effect, trading a system makes you a robot, and that's not a place I would like to be.

Neal: You are bound to upset a lot of software vendors out there who sell back-testing programs.

Phantom: I'm sure that some readers of this book have developed trading systems and have profitably traded them over a large sample size of trade and are probably snickering at my opinions on trading systems. I'm just saying that mechanical systems do not fit into my psychological framework. If mechanical systems fulfill your psychological requirements and you are able to take every trade without the slightest deviation, and you are consistently profitable, then more power to you.

Neal: What about combining a system with trader savvy?

Phantom: Personally, I don't see how you can combine the two. Being a system trader is like being pregnant; either you are or you aren't. There is no gray area. Once you start injecting subjective judgments into the decision process, then your system becomes worthless because the hypothetical trading results of your back-test are predicated on taking every trade without second-guessing the trading signals. For most individuals, I feel it is probably impossible to take every trade generated by a mechanical system. Markets are so dynamic and chaotic that systems will "work," then "stop working," and then start "start working" again. It is extremely difficult to continue trading a system when it is not working because the actual drawdown inevitably exceeds the largest hypothetical drawdown you have back-tested and doubts begin to arise as to whether the system is permanently flawed. Once these doubts enter your mind, you are finished as a system trader because you will temporarily or permanently stop trading the system and start designing a new one, only to repeat the cycle all over again, just like a dog chasing its tail.

Neal: But what about a simple breakout system?

Phantom: The problem with breakout systems is that this methodology is utilized by most off-the-floor traders, including some very large fund managers. This has given rise to the infamous "false breakout," as hundreds of traders spot the same 15- or 20-bar breakout and enter at the same time, only to find that they are the only ones buying or selling and then watch prices reverse to stop them out. This is very damaging psychologically, and financially, as 65 to 70% of your trades will be losers. You must have the mental and monetary stamina to endure this type of torment if you decide to trade breakouts. A high percentage of losing trades indicates you will have a long series of consecutive losers in a row, and if the series of losers is long enough, it will force many traders to throw in the towel. Eventually, that big coffee or bean move will come to bail you out, but the question is, if that big move comes later rather than earlier, will you still be in the game? Unfortunately, computer dependency has replaced common sense and made many individuals both mentally and physically lazy. That's why I keep my own hand-drawn charts, because I know that very few traders have the time, inclination, or energy to do likewise, and I always like to do what everyone else isn't doing. When I have a losing trade, I don't blame any "system;" I blame myself and analyze the trade to discover what I did wrong and whether I can avoid a similar situation in the future. Unfortunately, nearly all traders, including the readers of this book, have minimal or nonexistent money management skills and are basically trading system addicts. You must master three disciplines to succeed in speculation:

1. Trading methodology
2. Psychological development
3. Money management

Most traders become fixated on and obsessed with the trading methodology and completely ignore the other two disciplines. This situation has not gone unnoticed by some clever marketing individuals and has given rise to the proliferation of seminars and trading system vendors selling questionable material for thousands of dollars. Unfortunately, as most of the individuals who purchase these products eventually discover, you cannot buy trading success.

Neal: Can you show some real-world examples and actual trades?

Phantom: I don't use trading software. Every individual has his or her own unique personality makeup regarding risk and reward. When you use someone else's trading software, you are trying to force their risk/reward outlook, which is designed into the software, into your personality, sort of like putting the square peg into the round hole. That's probably why traders invariably try to modify a trading system they have purchased by changing the stop-loss or profit parameters. The personality that designed the software was different from theirs so they try to bend the trading parameters to fit their own psychological makeup. Developing a trading methodology should be like buying a suit. You purchase a suit that fits your own height and weight, not someone else's. Don't try to fill out a suit designed for Arnold Schwartzeneggar. I wrote The Manager software in Quickbasic language. It is a simple, no bells and whistles program that provides me with all the money management statistics I require.

Neal: What seminars do you attend? What publications do you read?

Phantom: I don't attend seminars, subscribe to publications, or have any favorite speakers. I figure if anyone possessed anything worthwhile, she or he wouldn't be selling it. My favorite book on trading is also everyone else's favorite, Jesse Livermore's biography, *Reminiscence of a Stock Market Operator,* by Lefevre. It's a fascinating look into the psychological aspects of speculation. My favorite nontrading author is Hemingway, probably for his straightforward, precise style of writing, which is the same way I try to analyze a market. I also like Kerouac and Thomas Merton.

Neal: There are plenty of seminar promoters and software vendors who are glad you do not get too much publicity. In recent years a lot of money has been made by selling trading systems. Maybe the cause is that we are too lazy and want the computer to do all the work.

Phantom: Anyone can design a trading system which will be profitable if back-tested over 5 or 10 years. Unfortunately, there is no guarantee it will continue to be as profitable in the future. There are countless stories of trading systems "not working" as soon as they are traded in real time. I would guess this is the reason most trading system sellers don't trade the method in a model account. It might be too embarrassing.

Neal: This interview will certainly create a lot of controversy. What specific information can you give the Chicago-style trader?

Phantom: Let me cover this with a series of points.

1. To succeed in speculation, you must play *defense,* not offense.

2. There has never been and never will be a Super Bowl champion that ranked in the bottom 20% of league defensive statistics.

Teams with porous defenses that give up lots of points never become champions. Offensive units can never score enough points to overcome the deficit created by a defense which continually gives up too many points. The most successful teams in all sports always field a defense which ranks in the top 20% of league defensive statistics. Many times, they are the best defensive unit in the entire league. Likewise, in speculation you must focus on *defense,* not offense. If you are not focused on defense, you will never become a truly successful speculator. The primary goal in speculation is not to make money. *The primary goal is capital preservation. Capital preservation is skillful psychological and financial management of losing trades.* Capital preservation is defense.

Neal: So it is capital, profits, and risk, right?

Phantom: The primary focus is the percentage of capital and the percentage of profits you will lose if your trade proves to be unprofitable. Will you be risking more than 2 to 3% of trading capital on the next trade, and if so, why? If your profit center currently has $10,000 in net income and your contemplated trade will lose $9000 if it proves to be unprofitable, how will this affect you psychologically, especially if it took 20 trades and two months to earn the $10,000 profit? You *must* play defense. Never lose more than 2 or 3% of trading capital on any trade unless you are in a high-risk/high-reward situation. Unprofitable trades are points given up to the other team. Profitable trades are points scored. If you have a poor defense and surrender too many points, your offense will never be able to score enough points to overcome the deficit. *A great offense will never negate a poor defense. This type of team will always fail.* Once a team gets behind because it continually gives up points, the offense slowly but surely starts to panic and discards its game plan. Now they must play catch up. Their carefully thought-out game strategy is thrown out and the team resorts to predictable and undisciplined play. You can see this occur every Saturday and Sunday during college and pro football seasons. You also see this unfortunate situation repeated in the field of speculation. Losing trades are too large and the trader begins to panic and abandons his overall trading strategy. He tries to catch up with his offense by overtrading to make up his losses. But no offense can make up for a poor defense. His trading becomes undisciplined and emotional, and like the harassed quarterback, he starts to throw interceptions instead of touchdowns.

Neal: Your use of sports and betting are great. It seems that sports betting and trading are quite analogous. Did observing sports betting help you?

Phantom: Ninety-five percent of sports bettors are long-term losers. That is a fact. However, I was fortunate enough to meet a few select individuals who were consistently successful in their wagering activities. I was intrigued by these successful individuals and became curious as to why they were succeeding in an enterprise where nearly everyone else failed. I discovered that the one common trait all of them shared was a very meticulous record-keeping system. Over the years, they had all developed numerous handicapping techniques. As a new season began, each handicapping technique was funded with a beginning bankroll, and key statistics were calculated for each technique after a bet was made. The beginning bankroll was updated after each bet, going up if the bet won and going down if the bet lost. After approximately 20 or so bets were made for each handicapping method, some techniques would be doing poorly, some average, and some would be hitting a high percentage of winners. Basically, a bell curve was formed. Out of say 20 techniques, 5 would be doing poorly—the left tail; 5 would be very profitable—the right tail; and 10 would be in the middle—marginally profitable or unprofitable. The bettor would then bet aggressively (usually the Kelly %) the five handicapping systems which were doing well and not bet (or even bet against, i.e., fade) the five systems which were doing poorly. Without realizing it, these bettors were using the profit center approach to wagering. Each handicapping technique was a profit center with its own bankroll. The statistics which were calculated after each bet revealed which centers were profitable and which were not. Bets were made only where the bettor had the edge. Anxiety, fear, greed, and uncertainty were significantly reduced or eliminated. These bettors knew exactly when, where, why, and how much to bet. What a different approach when compared to the average bettor, who had no idea how much to bet or who to bet on. These long-term losers relied mainly on hunches and their bet size amounted to whatever "felt" right. I mentally drew a comparison between the two types of bettors:

Winners	Losers
Calm, in control	Extremely emotional
Disciplined	Undisciplined
Confident	Anxious
Organized	Disorganized
Excellent record-keeping	Nonexistent record-keeping
Businesslike approach	Like the action and excitement
Professional, winner	Amateur, habitual loser

Neal: There is an amazing parallel between wagering and trading.

Phantom: There was no doubt in my mind as to which group nearly all traders belonged, including myself. I was determined to extricate myself from the right-hand column and become a citizen of the left-hand column.

Note: You can reach the Phantom by contacting Neal Weintraub; he will forward your message.

Pit Stops

THERE's GOTTA BE RULES

These rules were given to me by my first clearing firm at the Chicago Board of Trade.

1. Practice your trading. The first hundred trades are the hardest.
2. Do not overtrade. It's best to begin with one lots.
3. If you are caught taking more units than you can handle, immediately get out of excess.
4. Use discomfort to your advantage. It may never go away.
5. Work on each trade. Don't lay back.
6. The ability to let a profit run is a developed skill.
7. Try not to be habitually bullish or bearish.
8. Never add to a losing position.
9. Learn quirks of other traders and brokers.
10. Watch disciplined traders. Try to model yourself after them.
11. Continuity is important; don't leave the pit.
12. Work on one or two reasonable goals at a time.
13. Be more interested in establishing a working pattern than making it big on one trade.
14. Spreading generates economic advantage and informational edges.

C.V.

WHY YOU DON'T NEED REAL-TIME QUOTES

C.V. is a real trader. We agreed not to use his real name. He does not want the publicity, nor, frankly, does he need it. He makes his living trading. I have three years of his trades. All are real-time trades. I first talked with C.V. when he lived in Washington, D.C. I saw his account statements and tried to urge him to trade a fund. Today, he lives in upstate New York overlooking a quiet lake in an historical home (circa 1830) that he and his wife are renovating. You will not find C.V. on any news group. Want to meet a trader who really trades from home and makes a living at it? Here is a rare opportunity.

Neal: When did you first get interested in trading?

C.V.: At about the age of 28. I recall reading an article on futures trading in *The Wall Street Journal*; in fact, there was a series of articles about a number of financial professions. At the time, I was a young lawyer with a wife and two children to support. So I knew that was not the time, but it was something I always wanted to do.

Neal: So you are in reality a full-time futures trader?

C.V.: Yes.

Neal: You must get some interesting reactions from people here in Washington?

C.V.: It's not a common profession. Most people consider it extremely risky. When I told friends and colleagues I was retiring from my law practice to become a futures trader, many were aghast.

Neal: What I find so fascinating is that we are conducting an interview while you have 50 deutsche mark positions on. Each tick represents about $600.00.

C.V.: My trades are long-term trends. I don't follow the markets tick by tick.

Neal: As I look around your office, I don't see a television with 24-hour news. I don't even see a price screen.

C.V.: I basically use the Internet to get price quotes.

Neal: Many of the quotes are delayed 10 minutes or more.

C.V.: True, but when I need a real-time quote, such as right after a major report, I can get it through a dial-up service.

Neal: You must have a lot of confidence in your trading system.

C.V.: Yes, I do.

Neal: What is the basis of your system?

C.V.: I use a breakout system as the basis for my trading, but the key to the system is risk management.

Neal: What is the actual name of the software?

C.V.: I use a software program called Trading Recipes. It allows me to write my own systems and to test an entire portfolio of commodities and futures rather than one at a time. It also allows me to determine how much risk I should run by testing the relationship between trade size, return, and drawdown.

Neal: You don't hear too much about Trading Recipes.

C.V.: That's because they don't do a whole lot of promotion, and Bob Spear, the guy who developed it, now trades a multimillion-dollar commodity fund.

Neal: You are one of the few traders who have allowed me to analyze your statements for the past three years, and I see that you have been consistently profitable.

C.V.: That's right. I consider myself very fortunate.

Neal: Recently, you did a presentation for an investment group. As you know, I modified it and called it "Tickle Me."

C.V.: Yes, I recall that.

Neal: I think our readers would benefit from this simple system.

C.V.: Recently, I prepared a report on a simple intermediate-term breakout system for my local trading group. The focus of the report was the importance of risk management in following a trading plan, but the system itself, based on historical testing, appeared to be tradable. The report is reproduced below.

RISK VS. RETURN

- Trading offers exceptional returns as well as a high degree of risk.

- Concentrate on managing the risk. The returns will take care of themselves.

- All technical analysis is based on a study of market history. The study should have a high degree of replicability in real time.

- To assure historical studies can be replicated, trade liquid primary markets. You need at least six or seven for diversification. The 10 markets in my portfolio are ED, TY, US, DM, JY, CD, CL, NG, C, and CT.

- Trade a simple system with the same parameters for all markets. This protects against the situation of a system working well on historical data and failing in real time.

MANAGING RISK

- Management of risk is achieved through proper sizing of each new position in terms of the system's risk profile and the risk-reward preference of the trader.

- The most important formula in trading is the Kelly formula. Kelly allows you to evaluate the amount of risk a system can absorb.

Where WP = winning percentage
       W = average win
       L = average loss

$$Kelly = ((WP * W/L) - (1 - WP))/W/L$$

For example, in a 50-50 coin toss where average win = 2 and average loss = 1

$$Kelly=((0.50^*2) - (1-0.50))/2 = 0.25$$

Return is maximized by risking 25% of equity on each coin toss. In comparing two systems with the same number of trades, the system with a higher Kelly can always produce a greater return at the same level of risk.

THE TEST-48 SYSTEM

I tested a 48-day breakout system with a 12-day trailing stop. Pinnacle Data Corporation continuous linked contracts were used for the period 1/10/91 to 6/30/96. I used my 10-market portfolio and allowed $60 for commissions and slippage. Testing was performed with Trading Recipes software.

The Test-48 system code consists of an entry stop and an exit stop.

```
Col1=Min[Low,12,1]; Col2=Max[High,12,1]
Col3=Max[High,48,1]; Col4=Min[Low,48,1]
Trade entry:Buystop=Col3; Sellstop=Col4
Trade exit:Sellstop=Col1; Buystop=Col2
```

TEST-48 AND KELLY

The system was run on an equalized risk basis to determine Kelly. Equalized risk means that a fixed dollar amount of risk is allocated to each new position so that, for example, a corn position will have the same initial dollar risk as a T-bond position.

Risk can be measured in different ways. I used the greater of margin and new risk, which is the difference between entry price and stop.

TABLE 9-1

		Basic Data			
	W	L	WP	W/L	KELLY
1/91 to 6/96	115	159	42%	2.68	20.3%
7/96 to 6/97	33	29	53.2%	1.38	19.4%

	Risk-Reward Profiles			
	1/91 to 6/97		1/91 to 6/96	
RISK (% EQUITY)	CAR*	DRAWDOWN	CAR*	DRAWDOWN
2.0%	23.1%	16.5%	22.3%	15.2%
2.5%	29.7%	20.8%	29.7%	19.8%
3.0%	36.0%	25.1%	36.4%	23.8%
4.0%	48.2%	32.6%	51.1%	31.1%
5.0%	60.2%	39.5%	64.7%	39.0%
7.5%	91.3%	45.9%	100.0%	45.5%
10.0%	99.5%	60.2%	103.7%	52.6%
12.5%	126.3%	65.6%	90.2%	57.9%
15.0%	121.8%	73.0%	84.4%	62.5%

*CAR = Compound Annual Return.

TEST PROCEDURES AND RESULTS

The test procedure was designed to establish the risk-reward profile for the system. I started with risk per trade (determined as set forth above) of 2% of equity, roughly 10% of Kelly. This was increased in steps to determine effects on return and drawdown. Risk was evaluated up to the turning point in the risk-reward curve, as shown in Table 9-1. No new trade was taken if the existing risk in the portfolio (the difference between closing price of positions and stops) exceeded 50 percent of equity.

TEST-48 UPDATE

The original Test-48 runs were on 1/1/91 to 6/30/96 Pinnacle continuous contracts for C, CT, DM, CD, ED, TY, US, CL, JY, and NG. Long and short entries are on 48-day highs and lows, and exit stops are trailing 12-day lows and highs. Sixty dollars per contract is provided for commissions and slippage.

A full year of out-of-sample data is now available. Test-48 was run with 6/30/97 data using the original parameters. The out-of-sample period shows a somewhat enhanced winning percentage and a lower average win to average loss ratio, resulting in a slightly lower Kelly. The risk-reward curves were calculated for the entire 1/91 to 6/97 period.

Neal: Would you explain Table 9-1 a bit more?

C.V.: The table shows the relationship between risk per trade, which is a function of the number of contracts and stop, return (CAR, or compound annual return), and drawdown. Up to a point, increasing risk increases return, while also increasing drawdown.

When risk is increased past the system's ability to absorb it, return decreases and drawdown increases.

Neal: In reality, how much does this system make?

C.V.: Traded on a conservative basis, the system would probably produce a return in the 15% range.

Neal: You do use some commonsense trading concepts, like trading into a report, etc.

C.V.: I've learned from experience that it is hard to quantify the effect of major reports in historical testing. Therefore, I do not use an entry order on a big report day until after the report is out.

Neal: What is your definition of a trend up and trend down?

C.V.: A good simple definition of a trend is 12 consecutive closes above (or below) the trailing close from 24 days ago. The trend is then in effect and stays in effect until the close is below (or above) the trailing 24-day close.

Neal: Where are your real-time quotes?

C.V.: As I mentioned, I don't use a tick-by-tick trading system.

Neal: Just thought I'd throw in a trick question. In previous discussions, you talked about the book *Market Wizards*. Is there one particular chapter you found significant?

C.V.: The book was extremely informative. The chapter on Ed Seykota I found of great interest. Seykota basically says to stick with the trend. There is no deep mystery about trading futures.

Neal: Where is your television? I mean where is CNBC and all that information technology?

C.V.: The markets are a better source of information on what is going to happen in the markets than any news media.

Neal: Would it be fair to describe your trading environment as Spartan? You have no quote monitor and no television.

C.V.: I would prefer the word *focused*. As I mentioned, I use the Internet for my quotes. I find quote.com, which displays bar charts in any time frame, from one minute to one month, to be very valuable. I rarely look at commodity news. Price already reflects what comes out in the news. One computer is dedicated to the Internet, the other to historical testing and daily updates on my system.

Neal: What seminars do you attend?

C.V.: I have not attended any seminars, although I have read a number of books on trading. Early on, I decided I would develop my own systems. I started with simple analysis in my Quattro Pro spreadsheet, which I still use.

Neal: In your estimate, why do so many traders end up being net losers for the year?

C.V.: I saw a detailed study of approximately 100 traders. The information was supplied by their brokers. Only 5 percent of the traders were profitable. The principal reason for losses was that traders closed out their winning trades early and let their losses run. This is, of course, the reverse of the old maxim: *cut your losses and let your profits run.* Apart from this, most traders have very little knowledge of money management.

Neal: So you don't believe in day-trading?

C.V.: I think it's very hard to day-trade. There is a lot of random movement within the day time frame. There is a premium on speed, and it's very hard to compete with the floor traders while sitting at a quote monitor.

Neal: Would you comment on the Phantom's interview (Chapter 8) on money management and system trading?

C.V.: It's a very sophisticated approach to money management. I think that many traders would find it difficult to sort out their trades to that extent. I use one basic breakout system with three variations—fast, medium, and slow, by which I mean, a break-out range from 40- to 60-day highs and lows.

Neal: What have been the most important influences on your trading style?

C.V.: I mentioned the Seykota interview in *Market Wizards*. Another important influence was Ralph Vince, who has written three books on portfolio management and trade sizing. Vince's concept of sizing a trade, which he calls *optimal F*, is extremely aggressive. *F* is the proportion of equity you risk on each trade. Referring to the Test-48 studies, *optimal F* would be the peak of the curve for return, which coincides with extremely large drawdowns. However, it is important to understand fully the concept of trade size, the only factor in trading you have complete control of. I have learned a great deal from Vince's discussion of the relationship between risk and portfolio return. The risk-reward curve for any trader should be based on the trader's tolerance of drawdown. I find I have a smaller tolerance for drawdown in percentage terms now that I am trading a larger account.

Neal: Anyone else?

C.V.: The software Bob Spear wrote, Trading Recipes, has played a crucial role in my becoming a professional trader. The ability to test an entire portfolio and see how my system worked on an historical basis gave me a great deal of confidence. Risk management is actually something you can program, as I've illustrated in the Test-48 paper. There is another important aspect to portfolio testing: It has some built-in protection against curve fitting. I use the same systems to trade all the futures in my portfolio. I know that my systems aren't the best systems for T-bonds or corn or deutsche marks, but because the systems have been tested against a 10-future portfolio, I believe they are more robust. For example, T-bonds have been in a long-term uptrend for the last five years. If they were to go into a long-term downtrend, a system based on just T-bond data for the last five years might not be effective. My portfolio includes several futures, such as crude oil and the yen, which have had a pronounced downward trend over the last several years.

Neal: Have you ever used any of the more popular software, such as TradeStation or Metastock?

C.V.: No, I started using Quattro Pro. I felt it was better to learn the basics writing in fairly simple spreadsheet language. After a few years, it became clear that I needed software to handle a portfolio.

Neal: What sort of correlation do you find between your historical testing and real-time trading?

C.V.: I have found that invariably the return is lower and drawdowns higher in real time. If historical testing shows a maximum drawdown of 20%, I expect to have a higher drawdown. The rule of thumb I use is that tested drawdown represents only four to five standard deviations, and in real time you will quickly get to six standard deviations, so a 20% historical test drawdown could easily be 25 to 30% in real time. The same principle works in reverse with historically tested return.

Neal: In 1997 you had an eight-month drawdown. How did you react to that?

C.V.: No trader likes a prolonged drawdown, but they are an inescapable problem with long-term trend-following systems. My historical testing had shown a longer drawdown of 9 to 10 months, so I was mentally prepared for it.

Neal: Have you ever had a market make a limit move against your position?

C.V.: Yes, and it's not a pleasant experience. During the summer of 1997, I had a short position in corn. The market opened limit up on Monday morning through my stop. I am suspicious of Monday morning gap openings up, and I thought there was a good possibility that this was a move designed to shake out the shorts. I checked prices on my real-time dial-up service every 10 minutes. My position was in the September contract. After about 20 minutes, the December contract came off limit. At that point I knew I could lock in a straddle by buying December, but it seemed reasonable to wait for September to come off limit, which it ultimately did. It came down a couple of pennies and held. When it started back up again, I got out of my position. The whole process seemed to take most of the trading day, but as I review my trading log, I see that I had completely liquidated my position within one and a half hours of the market open.

Neal: Do you have any advice for someone contemplating a career in trading?

C.V.: As is true in any profession, the best way to start is right out of college. Go to Chicago and learn about trading from the bottom up. Becoming a futures trader in mid-life is more complicated because of financial obligations. You should cover any and all financial obligations with nontrading funds. And what's very important is to take the time to learn to identify and trade trends. For the off-the-floor trader this is the most efficient method of trading. Don't try to day-trade the S&Ps. Do not buy a system; you are better off developing your own. Do not try to pick tops and bottoms. Finally, learn the basics of risk management. Remember, the size of your trade is totally within your control. Keep your risk small. A good rule of thumb is to limit risk per trade to between 2 and 3% of trading equity.

Neal: A number of people I have spoken to have stated they started trading futures because they did not have

enough money to trade stocks. Surely you must have some advice for someone who has these ideas.

C.V.: If someone has only $5000 available for trading, I do not think that person should be trading commodities. Using the risk-per-trade rule of thumb of 2 to 3% of trading capital means that $100 to $150 would be risked per trade. Most people will risk more than that, and their trading capital will be depleted. If that person has a burning ambition to trade commodities, he or she should go to Chicago and get an entry-level job in the business.

Neal: Do you always follow your system?

C.V.: Whenever I am in a trade, I always follow my system's exit signals. In fact, if my system says get out tomorrow on the opening, I will many times get out during the night session. I allow a limited amount of discretion in taking a trade. As I mentioned, I will not put an order in to initiate a trade before a big report. Sometimes I wait for confirmation before entering a trade. For example, if one of my systems is giving a signal to buy T-bonds but I have no other buy signal for T-bonds or T-notes, I'll wait for a second system to kick in before taking the trade. I will never take a trade which is not based on a tested system.

Neal: I noticed you failed to take a short position in corn this summer. Isn't that contrary to your system?

C.V.: For my breakout systems, avoiding a short corn position in the summer is statistically preferable. This would be true even adding 1998 to the database. The reason is that my trailing 12-day stop gets hammered by the "shake the shorts" rallies, such as the limit move I discussed. My systems would have a positive '98 return, which would not offset the prior years' losses. To trade corn short in the summer requires a different type of stop strategy.

Neal: Even though you're a system trader, I noticed that in a recent trade you exited a position early before your trailing 12-day stop was hit. Could you elaborate?

C.V.: I have found a trailing 12-day high/low stop to be very effective trading intermediate-length trends, which typically end with a consolidation period. Several years ago, I realized that under special circumstances, such as a blowout top, the 12-day stop left too much money on the table or resulted in excessive volatility in my account. I therefore developed an analysis of circumstances where a combination of increasing (or decreasing) price plus increasing volatility made it likely that an extreme top (or bottom) was forming. Historical testing showed that it was possible to identify such circumstances often enough to make it worthwhile to incorporate an exit strategy based on the analysis into my systems. The objective is not to pick an exact top or bottom, but to exit prior to the excessive volatility that often accompanies market extremes.

Neal: If you look at the various steps in trading, order entry, money management, trade exit, and choosing the correct market, how would you rank them in terms of performance?

C.V.: Choosing the markets to be traded is crucial. You must trade liquid markets to trade successfully. Such markets exhibit consistency over time. They are also less risky. An illiquid market such as orange juice can have limit moves for three or four days in a row. The only highly liquid market I do not trade is the S&P. There are two reasons for this: First, I consider the stock market itself a vehicle for long-term investment measured in years, rather than speculation measured in months. Second, the S&P does not trade like any other liquid futures market. I find more correlation between the trading characteristics of corn and T-bonds than between T-bonds and the S&P. Of course, when I started trading, the S&P margin was around $12,000. Since I consider margin the minimum risk on a trade, that meant that I should not trade the S&P, using a 3% risk criteria per trade, until I had approximately $400,000 in my account. The e-mini S&P contract has reduced risk per contract to more manageable proportions. Even so, with a current margin requirement of approximately $3300, you would need over $100,000 in your account to trade one e-mini contract. Once the markets have been selected, there are three parameters to be considered: trade entry, trade exit, and risk management. Trading literature focuses to a large extent on trade entry. Pick up any issue of *Stocks and Commodities* and you will find at least one article on trade entry. Invariably, trade entry is predicated on getting aboard a trend at an early stage. My opinion is that trade entry contributes about 20% to trading success. Whether you enter a trend on a breakout or a moving average crossover or a more exotic approach is not important. What is important is to trade with the trend. When the train is moving, you should be on board.

Neal: How would you rate exit?

C.V.: I would weight trade exit strategy's contribution to success at 30%. The most crucial time in a trade is the two-week period following entry. If the trade is going your way, you don't have to worry. If the trade moves against you, however, you must face the question: Where do I get out? Many traders do not like to take a loss, but losses are part of trading. The important point is to minimize the loss. Referring to the Kelly formula I described above, the ratio of average win to average loss is just as important as the winning percentage. I have found the concept of maximum adverse excursion, which was developed by John Sweeney, to be very useful. He has written about it in *Stocks and Commodities* as well as in several books. In essence, he says to test how far a trade can move against you before it becomes a loser. Trade entry and exit together account for 50% of trading success. The other 50%—the single most important factor—is risk management. There's an old saying in trading: If you don't control your risk, they'll carry you out. Many traders starting out emphasize trade entry, and to a limited extent, trade exit, but do not devote sufficient attention to risk management. I should not be unduly critical of beginning traders when it comes to risk management. The recent experience of Long Term Capital Management, in which a $4 billion hedge fund incurred a 90+% drawdown, suggests that even the most sophisticated traders may not utilize appropriate risk management techniques.

Neal: Why are you so big on risk management?

C.V.: The ability to control risk is critical to staying the course. As we've discussed, 1997 was a difficult year for me, with an extended drawdown. By controlling risk, my equity was preserved to capitalize on winning trades. I can't predict when a good trend trade will come along, but I do know from historical testing that I need to preserve my capital until it does.

Neal: Where do you come up with new trading ideas?

C.V.: When I first started trading, I read a great many books to gain an understanding of the markets. Now that I've been trading for a while, I find that I frequently generate ideas. Perhaps one in ten will offer a measurable improvement to my existing systems, and of these, only a fraction will wind up being incorporated into a system. The markets are not static. They evolve over time, and my trading systems have likewise evolved in an effort to keep pace.

Neal: Why not consider day-trading when you see simple trading opportunities?

C.V.: I believe day-trading is very difficult for the off-the-floor trader. I have tested some ideas but have found it difficult to achieve the same degree of profitability inherent in intermediate- to long-term trend systems. The problem with day-trading is that the maximum profit is limited by the day time frame, and the risk—the amount that must be allowed for a stop—is quite large in relation to the realizable profit. This means that the Kelly ratio I discussed above is relatively low. Let me illustrate: T-bonds have an average daily range of about 28 ticks. Suppose you find through testing that if T-bonds rise 12 or more ticks from the open and then come back through the open within three hours, they have a tendency to close below the open. On average, you can expect, at most, 16 ticks potential profit by placing a sell stop at the open (28-tick range minus 12-tick advance over open). In reality, your potential profit will be 10 to 12 ticks unless you can pick the exact bottom for the day. To gain this much, you must risk the random intraday movement of the bond market, which I estimate at 6 to 8 ticks. On every trade, you have to pay the bid-asked spread of 1 tick on entry and exit, plus brokerage commissions of half a tick. The profit potential is reduced by $2\frac{1}{2}$ ticks to $7\frac{1}{2}$ to $9\frac{1}{2}$ ticks, while the loss is increased to $8\frac{1}{2}$ to $10\frac{1}{2}$ ticks. The average-win-to-average-loss ratio is likely to be less than 1. Referring again to Kelly, you're going to have to have a very high percentage of winners to overcome the average win/loss handicap. Using the Test-48 Kelly of 0.2 as a benchmark, you would need 60% winners with a win/loss ratio of 1 to match it. With a win/loss ratio of 0.8, you need 65% winners to get a 0.2 Kelly. If you can develop winning percentages this high, your rewards will be far greater in intermediate- to long-term trend trading.

Neal: What happens if markets stay in a trading range? You might not be able to trade trends. Do you have a backup plan for nontrending markets?

C.V.: I initially selected the markets I trade by looking at historical weekly charts. Most of the markets I trade have at least one, and often two tradable trends each year. They have continued to exhibit these characteristics during the period I have traded. While the possibility exists that one or more of the markets will go into an extended trading range, I have as yet seen no signs of this.

Neal: Speaking of day-trading, I thought you might enjoy Mark Brown's response to a new trader asking about day-trading the S&P.

C.V.: Sure.

Neal: In the e-mail, Mark stated the following: "You actually have a better chance to win a lottery than to become a long-term year-after-year day-trader of any commodity. When you throw in the idea of doing this on the S&P, your odds go from winning the lottery once in a while to winning the lottery every week for 10 years straight. I suggest that you limit yourself to a specific amount of money to lose. Now, take the rest of the money and give it to a trustee who will not allow you to have it once you blow the account." These are Mark's comments, not mine. But I cannot help see how they mirror your sentiments. Thanks for the interview, C.V.

An author comment: The above interview with C.V. is one of the more important interviews of this book. C.V. understands that trading Chicago style is understanding how the pit works and that patience, money management, and a plan are the same elements we use in Chicago. It is merely the time frame that is different.

You will note that there are a few interviews where there are no e-mail addresses or Web sites for further information. This interview is one of them. C.V. continues to trade the markets, and quite frankly, that is all he wishes to do. However, you may contact me, and I will forward your e-mails to him.

The figures that follow (Figures 9-1 through 9-6) are examples of the types of contracts C.V. trades. Note the tendency of contracts to develop strong trends without huge spikes.

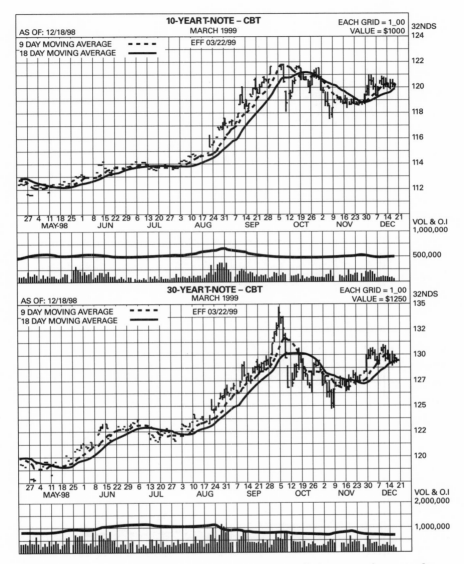

FIGURE 9-1. In both of the above markets, C.V. pulled out significant profits.

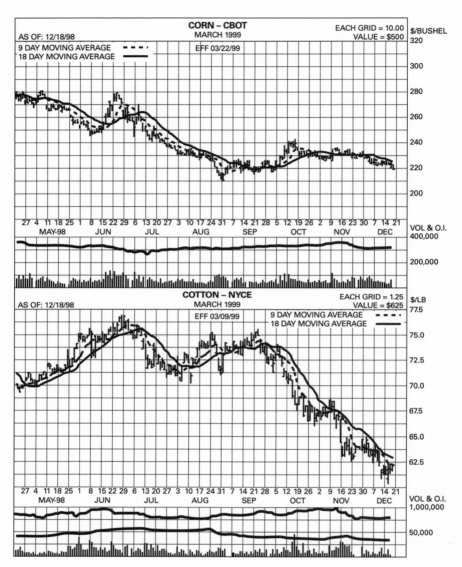

FIGURE 9-2.

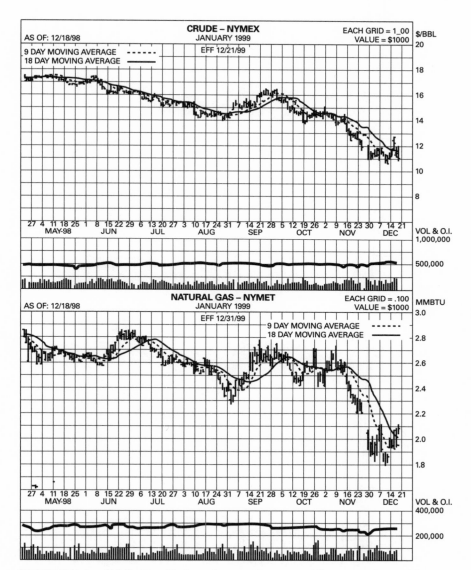

FIGURE 9-3.   While New York markets tend to cause Chicago traders to shy away, crude oil and natural gas are strong trend leaders. The objective is to wait for the trend.

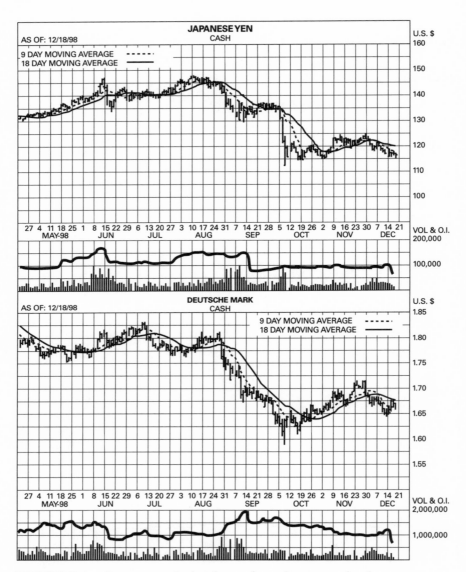

FIGURE 9-4.   Once currencies break out of a trading range, they have a tendency to run quite a while in one direction.

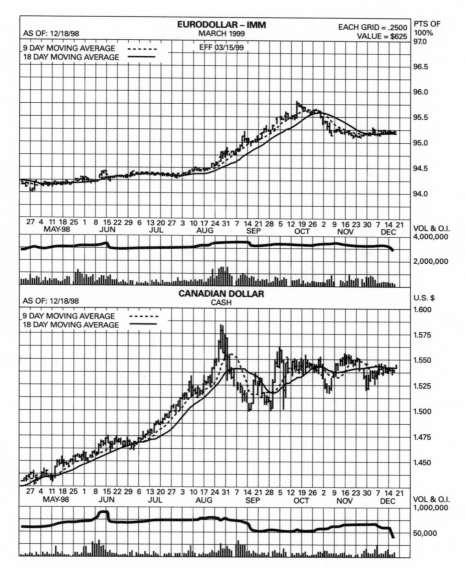

FIGURE 9-5.   With a breakout system, patience is the operational word.

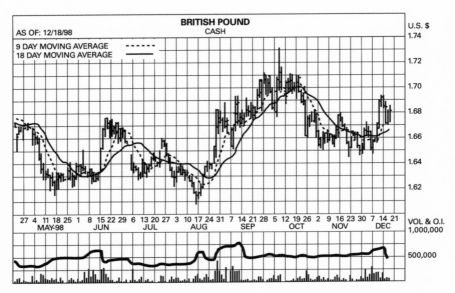

FIGURE 9-6. Here is an example of why C.V. does *not* trade the British pound—only one or two good trades.

MICHAEL CHALEK

SOFTWARE WITHOUT TEARS

Michael Chalek is a computer-modeling expert and system developer in the futures and stock markets. His trading systems have been featured in such publications as *The Wall Street Journal, Forbes, Technical Analysis of Stocks and Commodities,* and *Futures* magazine.

Mr. Chalek attended the University of Illinois and received a B.S. degree in electrical engineering. In July of 1979 he received a graduate M.S. in electrical engineering. Mr. Chalek has also done additional graduate studies in microprocessor theory and design, leading toward a doctorate in electrical engineering.

Neal: How did you get started in this business?

Mike: I began trading the stock market shortly after graduating from the University of Illinois in 1973. At the time, I did not know what a bear market was or that we were in one. My inexperience led to some very gut-wrenching experiences with several stocks. I knew nothing of selling short, just of buying stocks. I accumulated shares in Teleprompter, Combustion Engineering, Pizza Hut, Williams Company, and a few others, along with the advice of an inept stockbroker. Within six months I lost my entire savings of $5000. It was time to hit the books. My first encounter was Nicholas

Darvas' *How I Made $2,000,000 in the Stock Market.* It was actually the best book to start with. Both sides of the trading equation (technical and fundamental) were touched on. With my engineering background, it didn't take me long to go with the underlying principle of technical analysis for possible trading success. I moved on to other technical books, such as *Technical Analysis of Stocks and Commodities* and Joe Granville's *A Strategy of Daily Stock Market Timing.* During the winter of 1977 I went to the Chicago Stacks (exchange libraries) after work, and painstakingly, by hand, I proved Granville's theory of balance volume, using all the Dow Jones stocks in the 1929 *Wall Street Journal.*

During 1983 I received a phone call from an individual (Allen Ko) who had read an article about me and was interested in some of my work. Over the course of about two years, Ko and I became good friends, and soon we codeveloped a system involving an adaptable volatility variable and a unique price pattern. Between the years of 1984 and 1987, Ko parlayed $25,000 into more than $2,000,000. I probably only made about $500,000 during that time. My discipline in trading was not as good as his. Sticking to a system was extremely hard, especially during the drawdown periods.

Neal: So what exactly is Dual Thrust?

Mike: Dual Thrust is a function of dynamic volatility and a unique price structured pattern which, when used collectively, gives inherent support and resistance levels in the market. We are looking for a breakout with either of these points and treat the signals as a stop and reversal methodology. The system appears to work rather well on the S&P intraday charts using time periods of 30 minutes or more.

Neal: Could a pit trader use it?

Mike: A pit trader could possibly use it if he had a computer on the side using, say, one- to two-minute bars. This would only be good for a fast scalp. Not much could be said for a fundamental trader because this is mathematical methodology.

Neal: What should traders look for when choosing software?

Mike: Choosing software to trade is a very tricky task. Do not rely solely on such third-party reviews as Futures Truth. They are only part of the equation. The user should ask the software provider what the data source was when the software model was back-tested. This might also reveal such things as whether the developer used actual contract data as opposed to continuously generated contract data. I have found vast differences when applying the two approaches. My software has a rollover feature which painstakingly applies actual contract data and will ask the user when to roll-over into the expiration month. TradeStation does not provide that kind of option. Watch out! The aspect of drawdown can mean different things to different people. I have found that some software developers actually use closed-position drawdown and do not mark to market-open drawdown, which simulates a real-life situation. A good software package will provide an ASCII data option, since most data vendors allow you to convert their particular format into ASCII data. This is a universally accepted data format which can be readily imported into any text editor.

Neal: And what about the developer?

Mike: Developers should provide full disclosure of their methodologies. Avoid those "black boxes." I have found that most vendors generate their code into a black box when they are either copying a strategy from a book or curve-fitting a specific trade occurrence somewhere in the past. By generating a "white box," the end-user will experience a higher comfort level. Otherwise, you simply can't trust the software. In addition, if the programmer had errors in the software, you would have no way to cross-check his results. It is important to know how many parameters the system is using. Anyone can take a methodology and curve-fit it to his or her liking by using an overabundance of variables to address a number of market conditions. These conditions will change in the future; they often do. I have found over the years that if a system has more than five variables, it falls apart soon after its release. Just peruse the *Futures Truth* rankings and see for yourself. Dual Thrust uses four variables, and I consider that the limit. As an extension to this argument, ask the developer to provide a three-dimensional profit curve for a wide range selection of his variables. This is a good way to visually see if you have a good robust model or just some isolated area of profit surrounded by an abyss of losses. In the February/March 1998 issue of *Futures Truth,* Dual Thrust was put to the real test. They applied it to 60-plus domestic and foreign markets. On top of that, they chose only one parameter set for all of the markets and found it to be a very robust system by performing in almost all of the markets.

The bottom-line real test would be for the purchaser of the software to ask the developer for any real-time results of anybody using the model. That should flush out about 90 percent of the noise factor. Unfortunately, with the advent of TradeStation, there has been a proliferation of software developers; the number has risen exponentially over the years. TradeStation has several bugs in it which have not been resolved to date. There is some Monday morning quarterbacking going on in that some unscrupulous developers have been taking advantage of this weakness. Supposedly, this is being taken care of in version 5.0. Therefore, the platform for developing the software model is very important to consider.

Another facet to the software model would be the amount of markets that it can trade. There are too many systems out there that only trade one market. A more robust system will trade several markets, although that could be considered by some to be a form of overoptimization.

Neal: Where can people reach you?

Mike: They can reach me at (800) 315-3893. My e-mail address is wetradeall@aol.com. My Web site is www.tradefutures.com.

Pit Stops

CHARTS AND INDICATORS

What is trading Chicago style? For one thing it is an open mind. The following post on the net from a Chicago trader strikes a familiar chord.

> I was educated at the University of Chicago. I began in the physics and math department and ended up a graduate student in economics. I've heard all of these arguments before. In the mathematics department, the statistics classes, and the economics department, we again and again were taught that the market is random and that indicators and "drawing techniques" (chart formations, trendlines, etc.) are not market predictors and therefore are useless.

> I have news for all of the instructors who made these claims, and I'll relay it to you now. Just because you argue that they don't work does not mean they do not work. In my personal experience, they work. My work uses the oldest method of validation: my bank account. I've been a professional trader for years now. I use trading tools that you might classify as useless.

> Very early in my trading career, a friend took me a few blocks down Wells Street in Chicago to meet a fellow who had a one room cubbyhole office. This fellow had a tiny quote screen (an old Marketview) and a huge drafting board where he was busily drawing away. This man was a slave to his own methodology (to this day, I have never seen anyone else use or apply these methods). He was a very nice fellow, very quiet, and when the market slowed a bit, he asked me what I used to "figure" my trades. I told him briefly, and then he began to tell me what he used.

> He was updating an IMM Swiss franc chart, and he had kept handdrawn charts of the Swiss hourly charts for a few years (remember, the IMM currencies hadn't been trading that long back then). He told me that he was expecting a major buy in the Swiss franc that day and then

showed me his chart. He pointed and told me where it had to go to make his buy level "valid." I watched as the Swiss franc ticked to within two IMM ticks of his price, and then it reversed its down moves and began heading up in a rush. I asked him if he had bought any Swiss when it approached his "perfect" buying level. He replied that he would only buy Swiss francs at that one level, to buy at any other level would "negate" the trade. By the time I left that office that day, the Swiss franc had traveled over 100 IMM ticks higher from the level it touched, and still the man kept updating his hand charts.

On the way back to our trading room, I told my friend that I thought that man was not going to be around as a trader much longer, since he clearly couldn't "pull the trigger" on the trades he anticipated. My friend laughed and told me the old man had been around a long time, and then he changed the subject.

I ran into that old trader about 10 years later. I was managing money in an offshore fund, and he made an appointment with one of my money sources to meet me. When I walked into the room and saw him, he showed no surprise and did not let on that he knew me. At the end of the presentation, he ended up making a very large investment in my offshore fund. He asked me to dinner and we spent that night speaking about the recent market moves. At one point I asked him why he invested money with me that afternoon, and he told me that he knew I was very successful at trading currencies and though he had watched them closely for many years, he was not comfortable trading them; they did not move to his rhythm. I reminded him of the Swiss franc chart he had been updating that day in his office, and he smiled and told me the price of the entry level he had been waiting for that day. He told me it had not reached his level that afternoon, or the rest of the year, since the Swiss franc rallied nearly a thousand IMM points from that price.

I asked a friend who ran a local bank about the old gentleman and got a surprising reply: He was a major stockholder in a huge local company (well over $300 million), and his local real estate holdings were worth even more. I asked what the man did for a living and my friend told me he made his living "trading commodities." Over the years, this old gentleman has given me countless letters, papers, and handwritten manuscripts (all written from the late 1800s to just about the end of WW II) that he collected from his correspondence with other successful traders that he knew (the equivalent of today's newsgroups on trading, I suppose). He did not like the "new" approach to trading (mathematics-based and/or computer-derived) or the new "fake" commodities being traded (nationalized debt and stock baskets).

Every time I read someone making these points that indicators don't work or chart formations are statistically invalid, I shake my head. To the people performing those tests and making those points, they may be useless. But if a trader can use them and use them to make money, does it matter what someone else's statistics say? Remember, the world was thought to be flat for many centuries and that the galaxies revolved around the earth. Are we too "sophisticated" and knowledgeable now to make those errors in "truth?" Perhaps acupuncture is just mumbo jumbo that has been used for well over 2000 years in China. Or perhaps it produces its effects by manipulating something that we don't yet understand, as a recent set of studies by several physicists in the U.S. reported.

I'll end this long post by revealing that I don't use indicators in my trading. I haven't found any that I "trust." That doesn't mean I don't look at them as others show me how they use them. Nor does it mean I doubt that others make money using indicators. I keep refining my own techniques, adding a bit here and there. One man's random walk may be another man's indicator. They are only tools, and if you gave a wrench to a caveman, I doubt he would use it as you do now.

Best,

Tim Morge

TONY SALIBA

Been There, Done That in Chicago

Tony is a floor trader and president of International Trading Institute. He is a trading legend in Chicago with more than thirteen years of floor trading experience.

Neal: With all the significant changes taking place here in Chicago, the concept of trading Chicago style has certainly changed from the concept of simple pit trading. What is your view of this, Tony?

Tony: Coming from the options trading side, I have a different viewpoint from many of the traders in the Chicago marketplace. This is mainly due to the fact that fewer than one-fourth of Chicago floor traders are trading options, the other three-fourths I would group into futures (of all different instruments) and stock traders. Had you asked me that question two years ago, I would have said the "face of change" was already showing itself at the CBOE. This is because their handheld project, which began in late 1988 or early 1989, had remanifested itself as a viable alternative to straight, hand-to-hand, open-outcry pit trading where things have to be carded up. So even two years ago, it was evident to those trading at the CBOE that a major change was afoot.

The rapid pace of change that we're seeing here in Chicago in terms of the media and those news items that are at the forefront of the futures exchange is primarily due to the fact that there are other screen-based markets now on U.S. soil. In December 1996 you couldn't say that; that is, the Eurex project has been here less than two years.

This is a viable example in which U.S. practitioners can compare their Chicago style of trading, formerly only open outcry. For the broker or FCM, it means calling down to the floor, arbing into the crowd, getting a ticket, arbing back to the phone clerk, getting a ticket written up, submitting it to the clearing firm, and then giving the fill on the phone. So there was something to compare to, as opposed to Globex, which has been around for six years but wasn't working well due to its technology. It was a closed system. Now, Chicago traders and brokers have seen a working example and said, "Hey, I like this way of trading. It is very efficient and it reduces the paper flow." The time it takes to get fills and the propensity for errors are also reduced.

Neal: Many pit traders are scared. Seat prices are dropping. Many are thinking of going back to school to learn a new trade. Can they adapt to the new technology?

Tony: That's a topic for an entire chapter, but it's definitely an apropos point. However, that fact doesn't change anything I said earlier about the way Chicago style trading is moving. The point that you raise, Neal, brings to the table the question of whether the same people will be the engines driving the deep liquid markets that we have in Chicago trading today. That question is unanswered today because the exchanges (for the most part, the two futures exchanges in town), haven't addressed it. They've been blindsided by it completely. They've missed the boat, so to speak, to keep their liquidity engine readied for the future. Their engine is the capital and trading acumen of the men and women who stand in the pits on the floors of these Chicago markets every day. The leadership is detached from that engine, in that it assumes that it can fend for itself in respect to the future role of exchanges and the way they will be doing business.

Neal: That's a pretty controversial statement.

Tony: What you have are professionals, damn good professionals, who are absorbed, and rightly so, with the day-to-day, teeny-to-teeny, tick-to-tick business of making money, providing markets, creating the liquidity of their trading companies and individual sole proprietorships. What they're *not* in the business of doing is worrying about world trends, market trends, and how the sea change of that style of business may impact them. Some of them, not all, but most of them, don't have the capacity to forecast this, so they're leaning on their leadership. They're leaning on the boards and the chairmanships of the exchanges to worry about where the battleship is going. They're going to do their jobs on the battleship, but turning the battleship around is not the job of the people working in the pits. It's more the job of the leaders (some of whom are also working in the pits).

To get back to your question about the readiness of the floor population and the liquidity engine of Chicago markets, they are caught by surprise. As of today, they are in denial. A lot of them are upset with their leadership, "How could you put us in this situation, to be blindsided, where an XYZ system could almost instantaneously take the order flow away from our engine and put it on another engine, an engine which we—the components of that engine, the traders, market makers, and brokers of our pits—could be and should be participating equally in?" Your question speaks volumes on the problems we're having right now. Traders are asking, "Do I go back to school and learn another trade? Do I ready myself to sell cars or real estate in order to feed my family?" What's happening is that men and women who are, for the most part, already skilled to trade using this new technology are running away because their leadership has not embraced them and the technology simultaneously.

Neal: Who are the market makers of the future going to be? Will we need exchanges?

Tony: Our SBT discussions, which I've given for the past few weeks, have described the components of the market model. A number of different models are being used and adopted around the world today. The Electronic Communication Network (ECN) model sprang up and flourished for OTC stocks. Island, for instance, or Instinet represent liquidity without accountability, because you have a lot of these individuals you speak of on their Bloombergs, CQGs, pivotpoints, etc., and they're buying and selling when they get signals. That works really well when you have a critical mass, which I believe you have in a treasury bond pit or an S&P 500 pit or the Eurodollar crowd. Where it breaks down is in more obscure products, for which the market makers and traders on the floor have a quid pro quo agreement with the exchanges, and thus the CFTC and the SEC. They make markets even when the issues are illiquid issues or obscure issues, because that's their job if they're standing in the pits. Upon being asked to make a market, they have to buy or sell. They're fully accountable.

On the screen you *may* have liquidity. The people who say we don't need market makers because they'll make the market are right part of the time, but part of the time they'll be absent. In times of high volatility and in illiquid issues or more obscure issues where they don't want to play, they have a different degree of risk tolerance and they have a different sense of buffering the markets. When you have people buying and selling and have plenty of them present, you have liquidity on the screen. But when you have someone stuffed one or two times too many, in a row, then they'll start to back off and the market will widen. On the floors, you must make markets if you're standing there, so the widening of markets only happens in real extreme periods.

One of the issues that the exchanges currently have to address is providing for accountability, having a team of traders and market makers that will be responsible so we won't have dark screens in these illiquid times.

You'll have just as spotty bids and asks when the market is officially on a screen as you would today if you woke these guys up at 4 a.m. and asked them if they wanted to make the market.

Neal: Studies of commodities and stocks for the last few years look at open, high/low, and close for their studies. If the market's open 24 hours, there's no urgency to get out there; you just keep going.

Tony: Markets close at least one or two days a week (on the weekends). All markets have a certain time for clearing purposes so they can "mark to the market," or settle prices. Here they do tests for margin calls and margin requirements. You will have primary trading hours, and then you will have the after-hours trading to modify trading scheduling. We all had this discussion 10 years ago. I was on the board of directors at the CBOE at the time when Globex was first announced. CBOE was scrambling to see about doing linkages and joint ventures with exchanges in different time zones. The CBOE did a study on what it would be like to trade 24 hours, and basically we came up with one big problem. The exchange could pull it all off from its own standpoint, no real hurdles, but there was no way to get the staff to the exchange in the late shift because of public transportation not running during those hours. Also, there were security issues and domestic problems.

Now, with the proliferation of some solid technology that would allow for screen-based trading from your home or from your office, allowing for double duty, day and night, public transportation isn't such an issue. As the exchange becomes screen-based, you have less of a requirement for exchange staff to be present. What does 24-hour trading mean to technical analysis? You'll see a lot of asterisks representing values based on a classic closing time. We've had stocks trading past the normal New York closing time for years now. It's very difficult to see what is a close from the night before anyway. I think technical analysis takes the 4:00 to 4:10 EST close and then works backwards from there anyway.

Neal: When trading Chicago style, will there be a need to come down to the exchange?

Tony: I don't think the floors are going to close up. I want to preface that by saying that I don't believe that pit-style trading will cease to exist anytime soon. It's really a matter of how the leadership plays it right now. In my opinion, it was crunch time at the CBOT to make decisions regarding what they were going to do with their own Electronic Technology Project A, which is growing very rapidly after hours. It's a very lucrative business. To bring the camel's nose under the tent and have them trade side by side during the day was politically unfeasible as recently as three to four months ago. When I spoke on this topic a month ago in an interview with Steven Strahler of *Crains Chicago Business,* I said that if the CBOT makes a decision to put the Project A alongside of daytime trading, they could begin to coexist. If a critical mass gets on the screen, then the pits will have less importance. The reason this is all happening at the CBOT and the Merc is because they have not embraced technology like the CBOE. The CBOE already has electronic order routing to and from the pits. Therefore, that floor will not close as quickly, by a wide margin.

Neal: In a futures pit, when there are four prices at the same time in the same pit, like the S&P 100, an order seems to come in, and for some reason, those guys in the middle just never get a piece of it. A friend of mine from New York had a tough time breaking into the pit. He got so disgusted that now he trades at night, and no one cares who he is anymore. He doesn't have a chance to shmooz with the brokers or need to. I think the guys that have been trading at that level are worried. Could we really get buried when the markets outside see all of these magic numbers showing up and CNBC says, "It looks like a hell of a day!"

Tony: Practically speaking, the way it happens on the screen is that Ma and Pa Kettle hit a button and decide they want to put in a bunch of buy orders because they see a crossover on a technical point. There's either going to be a contraorder in the marketplace to turn their order into a trade, or there's not going to be anything there at all. If there's no contraorder (opposite side) available, their orders will either be kicked out, depending on the type of order they're using, or they will be put into the order book.

The big difference can be seen in a commodity example. Archer Daniels Midland trades in illiquid issues (grains, for instance), and they're working a thousand to buy. They don't just put the order in the crowd blindly; they usually give it to the best broker to work it, and that broker will nibble and take and nibble and take so as not to disturb the price too much. On the screen, the same thing will happen. They will have price points where they would be interested in buying a thousand, regardless. They might put their 50 lots or 100 lots in and nibble and take from the rest of the orderflow. Then, the Ma and Pa Kettle orders will seek that level. But, as the price runs up, alerts and alarms on trading terminals will be set off and supply will come to the market because the prices are outrageous.

Now that sounds like a volatile and loopy market, but the reality is that a lot of people are not going to wait until those alarms go off, and they will have their orders in the marketplace. So you have a very deep and rich string of sells cascading up in price and buys supporting down, depending on the product— and I'm talking futures. Options trading is different altogether. You'll see a fair and orderly market most of the time, but there are times when there will be gaps and people won't be sure which way to go or what values to use.

Neal: Your classroom teaches institutions. Where does a small trader go to learn this?

Tony: If it is a novice trader and he uses "the friendship network" to make money, he'll need to be retooled and taught the different strategies that will work on the screen. If it's an old-timer, like us, maybe someone who's had a lot of experience doing a good job down in the crowd, the learning is another dimension in the business. For instance, in futures trading, the number-one issue for the board of directors of the two commodity exchanges in town is whether they are going to lose their captive audience to some third party.

That captive audience consists of FCMs and their user groups and the exchange floor people. For the most part, all the exchanges are meeting places. They also guarantee those trades. They guarantee all of the financial infrastructure on both sides. But if one side or the other decides to go play somewhere else, then the second group is going to be disenfranchised. This would happen, for example, if the sell side (FCNs and their user base) went to a third-party system and decided that they were going to play there because the liquidity was already bought. It's up to the exchanges to take the positive aspects that their membership offers and retool that so that this doesn't happen.

Look at what futures traders do: They take on inordinately large amounts of risk. They are gamblers, speculators, and risk-takers . . . liquidity providers. They provide for the other side of the marketplace, so that the exchanges thrive. That's a lot more risk than a typical options trader takes on in any given day. Options traders look for relationships and take a smaller amount of risk for their part. What I've been saying for months is that the exchanges are not going to take everyone in the S&P pit and turn them into options traders. But if you can take the people in the S&P pit and point out to them that there are relationships, that when they go on the screen, those relationships form their "leans," then you're more than halfway to saving your liquidity providers.

You already mentioned technical and fundamental relationships in terms of price points. These individuals who already have an understanding of this can learn some of the dynamics of relative pricing, then go on the screen. They bring risk tolerance to the table. This is part of the exchanges' asset base.

Neal: The only other way, then, to take your courses is to come to Chicago?

Tony: Not necessarily; our computers will travel. We deliver at least a few programs out of the country each year. In the past, we delivered more, but most of the major banks in the screen-based trading community in Europe send their new people to us. It's a perk and "bomb-proofing."

We do have at least a few people in every class who are entrepreneurs. They want to get some practical experience with screen-based trading simulators. We combine the curriculum content with simulation, and it gives users a real business to take back with them. A lot of our graduates, be they individuals or traders for large institutions, meld something that they were already interested in with what we teach them. Therefore, they can continually look to two sides of the coin and realize that no one thing is always going to work for them. It's good to have that kind of backup.

Neal: What is your Web site?

Tony: It's www.itichicago.com.

NEAL WEINTRAUB

THE VALUE OF MY CAR GOES UP OR DOWN DEPENDING ON THE AMOUNT OF GAS I HAVE

The 17 questions traders most frequently ask.

Question 1: What were the first rules of trading you learned?

Neal: The first rules were given to me on a 3 x 5 index card. I still have copies in my possession.

1. Practice your trading. The first hundred trades are the hardest.
2. Do not overtrade. It's best to begin with one lots.
3. If you are caught taking more units that you can handle, immediately get out of excess.
4. Use discomfort to your advantage; it may never go away.
5. Work on each trade. Don't lay back. The ability to let a profit run is a developed skill.
6. Try not to be habitually bullish or bearish.
7. Never add to a losing position.
8. Learn the quirks of other traders and brokers.
9. Watch disciplined traders. Try to model yourself after them.

10. Continuity is important; don't leave the pit.

11. Work on one or two reasonable goals at a time.

12. Be more interested in establishing a working pattern than making it big on one trade. Spreading generates economic advantage and an informational edge.

These are still valid tips, but today I would add four more.

13. Know options and how and when to use them.

14. Never stop learning. Make sure that you are as good as your kids on the PC.

15. A trading system is only a model. It is not the real world.

16. If someone were to create a perfect trading system, that person would not sell it.

Question 2: I've heard of something called the trader's prayer. Is there such thing?

Neal: I have heard all kinds of prayers in the pits. The one I most enjoy is one I saw on a poster distributed by Futures Source, a cutting edge software company based in Chicago.

May I never be facing north when the market's headed south,
    and may locked limits always be on my side.
May the money left on the table be someone else's,
    and may my pockets be deeper than the correction.
May I always be five minutes ahead of the market,
    and may my runner have a clear path to the pit.
And if this one is a winner, I swear I'll quit.

Question 3: What is meant by "freaking out" when trading?

Neal: Well, that can mean a lot of things. According to Frank Zappa, the late wizard of our age:

Freaking out is a process whereby an individual casts off restrictive and outmoded standards of thought, dress, and social etiquette in order to express creatively their relationship to the immediate environment and social structure as a whole.

On a more serious note, freaking out means you lose control of your trading.

Question 4: What are the different types of memberships at the Chicago Mercantile Exchange and what are their costs?

Neal: Table 12-1 does a very good job of explaining the various memberships. Please note: They are subject to change.

Question 5: You say that traders will give different answers to the same risk-reward question. Can you explain?

Neal: Certainly. In one case, each person in a group of traders was handed $30 and told they could walk away with the money, or they

TABLE 12-1   Types of Memberships in the Chicago Mercantile Exchange

TYPE	CURRENT PRICE	COST TO LEASE	REQUIRED TRADING CAPITAL*
Full CME membership	$425K	$3000/mo	$50K
IMM division membership	$418K	$2800/mo	$50K
IOM division membership	$211K	$2200/mo	$50K
GEM division membership	$ 39K	$ 300/mo	$25K
Permit programs	Usually under $3K	n/a	—

* Leasing a seat has different capital requirements than owning a seat.

could take their chances on a coin toss, winning $9 more if the coin came up heads but losing $9 if it turned tails. About 70% took the gamble, knowing that they would end up with at least $21. Traders in another group were offered a slight variation. They could flip a coin, and heads would pay $39 and tails would pay $21. Or they could just take $30 with no coin toss. Only 43% chose the gamble. A little arithmetic shows that the two outcomes are identical, but the traders made different choices. Why? Because, as behaviorists note, it is not just the information that determines behavior but also how it is processed. That is mental accounting.

Mental accounting may explain why the 1987 market crash did not have the negative impact on the economy that pundits had forecast. Traders merely thought it was a correction, and so no panic.

Question 6: Can you explain the concept of spreading?

Neal: To explain spreading as a trading technique—and its importance to the liquidity and viability of futures markets—it is necessary first to understand the sources that give rise to market liquidity. The success of any market, especially a futures market, is dependent on its liquidity, that is, the bids and offers flowing into the pit. In markets, it is a common thought that the more bids and offers compete with each other, the narrower the spread between the bid and the offer. And the narrower the spread between the bid and offer, the more liquid and efficient the market. An illiquid market is one where the spread between bid and offer is wide. In such a market there are large price gaps between sales.

Be it electronic orders or floor orders, the more active the participation, the more liquid the market. Market liquidity will not always be enhanced because it exists on the Internet, or any other computerized delivery system. In fact, the E mini has liquidity because of the larger S&Ps.

There are only a few basic techniques for trading futures markets. They are used interchangeably by participants whether they are off or on the floors of the exchanges. These techniques are *scalping* (*market making*), *position trading,* and *spreading.*

The techniques of a futures market spreader are quite different from a scalper's or a position trader's. A spreader trades the differential between two or more contract months in a given commodity rather than the price of any given contract. In other words, the spreader will *go long* a quantity of one contract month and simultaneously *go short* an equal quantity of another month of the same commodity. Thus, his or her profit potential is based on whether the price of the commodity goes up or down, on the narrowing or widening of the differential between the contract months that make up the spread position.

Today, many spreaders perform this activity among three or four contract months at the same time. The objective is to pick up even the smallest increment of profit in the shift of the differential(s). The spreader is always alert to a new offer or bid in one given month that could spread profitably into another month. He is quick to react to any sudden "downdraft" or "updraft" in the market so that he can *unwind* one side of his spread for that small moment of market movement and *hook it up* again as soon as the price movement has stopped. The vast majority of spreaders apply this technique as a consequence of an accumulated open spread position. A spreader will usually have a theory, based on her analysis of market economics or dynamics, that a certain differential in a given commodity future will, over a period of time, narrow or widen.

Question 7: What is a scalper?

Neal: There are many types of scalpers. Some operate along classical lines by buying and selling between the smallest increment allowed by contract specifications.

In every case, the scalper attempts to flow with the immediate market movement, being among the first to sell as the market begins to fall and the first to buy when the market starts to rise.

Most often, the scalper liquidates a portion or his entire position as soon as the minor market movement has ended or as soon as he finds that his purchase or sale is in danger of turning into a loss. Thus, a scalper will institute and liquidate a small position many times during one day. Scalpers seldom leave the pit during trading. As a general rule, most scalpers keep only a very small, if any, open position overnight.

Scalpers are predominantly on-the-floor, member participants, since it is very difficult and far too costly for an off-the-floor participant to conduct this type of market trading. That is why it is difficult to day-trade off the floor paying retail commission.

Question 8: In 24-hour trading, what kinds of indicators do people use?

Neal: Time-based indicators are useless. Basing trading on high, low, and close does not make sense. I think *point and figure charts* and *market profiles* are of greater use to the 24-hour computer trader.

Question 9: What do you think of hedge funds?

Neal: Well, the first hedge fund was started by Edward Thorp. He introduced the public to counting cards in blackjack. His 1962 book, *Beat the Dealer,* is still a classic. He said unless you have an advantage you can exploit in trading, a hedge fund is merely a gamble. In short, you must focus on the model and know how it will behave when the market blows up. The problem with most hedge funds is that they are not hedged.

Question 10: Is there any one Web site that you think traders should have in their arsenal that is commonly overlooked?

Neal: Information is an essential for any fundamental trader. The Economeister Web site, located at www.economeister.com is a good source for market information.

On the home page, several news headlines related to major economies, monetary policy, currencies, bonds, derivatives, and other financial news are listed, along with an excerpt from the article. The full articles may be accessed by clicking on "more," located after each excerpt. Current articles listed on this page discuss the dollar/yen exchange rates, the producer price index, and the U.S. Treasury market. By selecting the "Today's Top Stories" icon located at the top of the page, you can access what this Web site deems the day's important news stories both in order of release time or by category. For a trader to be able to access a site that has gone through the vast amount of news information available and been narrowed down to market-related articles is vital in today's rapidly moving markets. The Web site also provides the user with an archive database with past articles back to November 25, 1997.

Another feature provided by Economeister that can prove very helpful is the "Global Calendar."

Question 11: How many on-line services do you have?

Neal: I have two services, Prodigy and a local service provider. Also, the Exchange has a Web site at www.cme.com.

Question 12: Why two services? Don't you think that's overkill?

Neal: Actually, no. There's no telling what may happen if one service goes down. There is always a need for a backup. And as you know, you can't always trust one service to work all the time, especially when you need a quote immediately.

Question 13: What software packages do you like?

Neal: First, I like the ones that are user-friendly. Software packages that require you to take classes or learn a computer language are doing a disservice. Buying software and then paying the developer money to learn it is a waste of time.

Question 14: What is the biggest mistake people make when purchasing software?

Neal: In my opinion, students buy software that requires too much time to learn. For instance, one software firm has a language that traders must learn in order to back-test. You also take classes to learn the software. In short, you develop programming skills at the expense of improving your trading. Traders who trade Chicago style are more pragmatic. They are not interested in learning programming language or the sorcery of back-testing. Why not purchase software that is compatible with the way you trade?

I am not saying one product is better than any other. Most are basically the same. I just take issue with claims that imply a particular programming language will propel you into the "traders' hall of fame."

Question 15: What is your opinion of day-traders?

Neal: That is a very hot topic these days. First, I am convinced that day trading should be done by those who get member rates or incredible discount rates. When you add in slippage, commissions, and short-term capital gains, the long-term trader clearly has the advantage. The apparent insouciant behavior of day-traders on television commercials frequently turns to irascibility when trading takes place in the real world.

Question 16: What trader do you think best represented Chicago-style trading?

Neal: I believe it was Charles P. DiFrancesca. He was a trader virtuoso and was known as the "Sultan of Scalp," the same way Babe Ruth was known as the "Sultan of Swat." You know, he never granted interviews or went on the seminar circuit. Why, he isn't even in the Futures Hall of Fame, yet he was a natural-born trader and risk taker. It was not uncommon for him to trade between 15,000 and 20,000 contracts a day. Most public speculators never heard of him. However, I would suggest people look up the book *Charlie P.,* by William D. Fallon.

Charlie made a video. I borrowed it and picked up some great points. Perhaps the single most useful item is to avoid a herd mentality. Another is to be a spreader. One more important point: Charlie believed that nobody invents anything new. He believed the best way to become a trader was to watch other people in the pits. In short, copy what other good traders do. That's why with all the new software and upgrades available, traders must know about spreads. He also had a goal: to be in the eye of the hurricane. It's the ability to be able to trade with chaos all around you and remain calm.

Question 17: Where do traders, or how do traders, create spread charts?

Neal: The most simple, direct way is to connect to the Web. Www.barchart.com offers an inexpensive means for spread-charting as well as three-legged spreads. What's more, the Web really represents the future of trading analytics.

Contact me (Neal) for classes and e-mail updates at thevin dicator@prodigy.net or at (800) 753-7085 (newsletter).

THE TRADE OF A LIFETIME

A trader who spent his life trading in Chicago is waiting to be admitted to heaven, while St. Peter is leafing through the Big Book to see if the guy is worthy of entering. St. Peter goes through the book several times, furrows his brow, and says to the guy, "You know, I can't see that you did anything really good in your life, but you never did anything bad either. Tell you what, if you can tell me of one *really* good deed that you did in your life, you're in."

The guy thinks for a moment and says, "Yeah, there was this one time when I was drivin' down the Lake Shore Drive and I saw what appeared to be a giant group of gang members assaulting this poor female runner. I slowed down my car to see what was going on, and sure enough, there they were, about twenty of 'em torturing this girl. Infuriated, I got out of my car, grabbed a tire iron out of my trunk, and walked straight up to the leader of the gang, a huge guy with a studded leather jacket and a chain running from his nose to his ear. As I walked up to the leader, the biker gang rapists formed a circle around me. Boy, was I ever scared.

So, I ripped the leader's chain off his face and smashed him over the head with the tire iron. Then I turned around and yelled to the rest of them, "Leave this poor innocent girl alone! You're all a bunch of sick, deranged animals! Go home before I teach you all a lesson in pain!"

St. Peter, impressed, says, "Really? When did this happen?"

The guy replies, "Oh, about two minutes ago."

LOUIS MENDELSOHN

No Market's an Island; Mendelsohn's "Method Behind the Madness"

Louis B. Mendelsohn is President and CEO of Market Technologies Corporation. His work in neural networks is gaining the attention of Chicago traders.

Neal: How do you think financial markets are different now from the last decade?

Louis: During the past decade, the financial markets have undergone an irreversible global integration. Whereas previously isolated from one another, they now function within a highly interconnected context. Now it is necessary for serious futures traders to factor intermarket dynamics into their trading decision-making. Traders who continue to focus internally on only one market at a time (single-market analysis), oblivious to the intermarket effects that related markets have on that market, are in my opinion putting themselves at undue risk.

It's no longer adequate to simply follow buy/sell signals generated from single-market trading systems. Such approaches, widely advocated in the 1980s and still popular today, fail to allow for individual differences in risk propensity, account capitalization, trading styles, and objectives. I now believe that such approaches are too inflexible and rigid.

Most important, they fail to account for decision-making inputs such as insight into market psychology, trading expertise, and rational judgment that only a human being can possess. Technical analysis results generated by today's trading software should be viewed as decision support information and cannot substitute for sound decision-making itself. It is foolhardy to think that an intelligent trader would ever want to turn over to his computer software the responsibility for making trading decisions.

Neal: That is a controversial viewpoint in light of system trading.

Louis: Traders assume needless risk when they restrict their analysis to a single market's past price history, no matter how much back-testing is performed or how many single-market indicators are examined. Now, I believe, the surest way to be successful on a consistent basis and to protect trading capital against large losses is to incorporate intermarket analysis into the trading decision-making process and for the trader himself to assume the active role of decision-maker.

Neal: Traders could use moving averages, though, right?

Louis: I believe most traders would agree that moving averages are an excellent tool for smoothing out short-term and random fluctuations in prices. However, traditional single-market moving averages are a "lagging" indicator because they are slow to react at turning points. They typically get in and out of trades after a change in market direction has occurred, often by several days, giving back profits and often turning winning trades into losers. In addition, there are serious pitfalls involving "curve-fitting" when reoptimizing the sizes of the moving averages. Another problem involves the occurrence of false signals during sideways or nontrending markets.

Neal: Tell me a little about your VantagePoint software.

Louis: Comprised of five neural networks, VantagePoint over-comes these limitations. One network predicts tomorrow's high, a second network predicts tomorrow's low, and a third network predicts a "neural index" based on a three-day moving average forecast. The fourth network predicts a five-day moving average for two days in the future, while the fifth network predicts a ten-day moving average for four days in the future.

VantagePoint's predictions are not based on a single-market approach that optimizes moving averages. Nor are its predic-tions linearly related to past single-market price activity. In-stead, VantagePoint takes into consideration the past ten years data from nine related markets that nonlinearly affect the mar-ket being traded. The result is a powerful "leading" indicator, comprising two predictive moving average crossover oscillators which, when viewed along with the neural index, gives the trader a clear indication of what the market is expected to do over the next one to four trading days.

VantagePoint's predicted intermarket information is de-tailed in an easy-to-read, one-page daily report, which is up-dated each day after the markets close. All you need to do is to collect the open, high, low, close, volume and open interest data by modem for the ten markets (target market plus nine related intermarkets) that comprise each VantagePoint program.

When the oscillators turn positive, VantagePoint expects the market to go up. Similarly, when the oscillators turn negative, VantagePoint expects the market to go down. Changes in the magnitude of each oscillator from day to day afford an early warning of an overbought or oversold condition and impending change in the strength or direction of the trend.

Depending on a trader's account capitalization, risk pro-pensity, and style, she can act on changes in one or both of the oscillators. She can either close out an open position if there is any indication of weakness, or only close out the posi-tion if the weakness exceeds a certain "threshold" amount, i.e., if one or both of the oscillators narrow by a minimum number of ticks.

The neural index is used to confirm these oscillators. It is based on a predicted three-day moving average of today's, tomorrow's, and the following day's closes. When the neural index is 1.00, VantagePoint expects the market to go up over the next two days. When the neural index is 0.00, VantagePoint expects the market to go down over the next two days. It presently makes these predictions with up to 78 percent accuracy.

A trader can also look at daily reports from related markets for additional confirmation. For instance, the Eurodollar, 5-year T-note, and 10-year T-note daily reports offer additional insight for bond traders into what VantagePoint expects to happen in the interest rate complex. Similar relationships exist between various energy markets, stock indexes, and currency markets that VantagePoint covers. The bottom line is that predictive intermarket information, based upon the pattern recognition capabilities of neural networks, offers traders a broader insight or "vantage point" (hence the name of the software) on the markets which can be realized by focusing solely upon the internal dynamics of each market alone.

Neal: So how can we translate this concept into profits?

Louis: Through financial forecasting incorporating intermarket analysis, traders can gain an anticipatory, not just a retrospective, vantage point on the markets. With single-market system testing, it's easy to discern where the markets have been and to discover simulated trading strategies which may have worked on past data. But the real payoff is in being able to anticipate future market direction consistently so that you can act decisively and confidently when real money is on the line.

With randomness and unpredictable events inherent in the financial markets, no one, regardless of financial, intellectual, and computational resources, will ever be able to make 100% accurate predictions. A maximum achievable level, in my estimation, is at best 80 to 85%. From a decision-making standpoint under conditions of uncertainty, even considerably less accuracy would offer an enormous competitive advantage over more traditional methods of analysis.

Neal: In some ways intermarket analysis is much like spreading. Would you say you're taking it to the next level?

Louis: Based on my experience of more than 25 years' involvement in the financial markets, and nearly as long as a commercial trading software developer, it is my opinion that intermarket analysis is on the brink of broadening the definition of technical analysis, just as system testing did in the early 1980s. The markets have changed drastically since then, and single-market trading approaches, although still popular, particularly among novice traders, now leave much to be desired. By incorporating predictive information based upon intermarket analysis into your trading plan, and by recognizing that success requires more than simply reading a trading signal off a computer printout or "eyeballing" price charts from related markets, you will become a more confident and effective trader in today's complex world of futures trading.

Neal: What advice would you give traders today?

Louis: Avoid the herd instinct. If the oft-quoted industry loss statistics (that 90 to 95% of individual traders end up as losers) are even remotely accurate, then to succeed, you can't just do what everyone else does. Otherwise, the most likely scenario is that you'll end up just like them. You've got to think, analyze, and act differently. After being involved with intermarket analysis for more than a decade, and with the world financial markets now more interconnected than ever, I believe that every trader needs to have at a minimum an awareness of what's going on in related markets. This is a critical piece of the analytic puzzle that can no longer be ignored if you want to avoid becoming a trading casualty. But overly simplistic intermarket analysis can be fatal, such as assuming that bonds and stocks always trade inversely with one another on any given day or hour. What we're talking about here is part science, part art. To be successful takes a lot of hard work. There is no easy fix. Traders who think so, who echo the grandiose claims too often made in this industry, are just kidding themselves—and will probably end up contributing to the industry loss statistics.

Neal: Can you show me some practical examples of how traders would use the output from your VantagePoint software program?

Louis: Sure. VantagePoint provides our clients with its predicted information in two ways. One is a graphical representation of the output in the form of a daily chart, and the other is a numerical representation of the output in a daily report. VantagePoint clients have the flexibility to look at this information either way, since some traders are more visually oriented, while others are more comfortable just looking at the numbers.

On the graph (see Figure 13-1), you can see the PTM (projected 10-day moving average) touching the TRNDM (actual 10-day moving average) at the bottom left. Each time those two lines converge and begin to cross, it is an indication that the market is about to change trend direction. When the two lines are moving together in an upward direction, VantagePoint is projecting the market to continue an uptrend. On the flipside, as the two lines begin to converge and move to the downside, VantagePoint is expecting the market to trend down. This occurred on this graph in mid-October. The PTM and TRNDM crossed to the downside, indicating to VantagePoint clients a change in market direction.

The numerical daily report (see Figure 13-2) has three sections. The first section is the index, which will be a number between 0.00 and 1.00. This indicates when the market is expected to make either a top or a bottom.

The main point traders look for on the index is an increase or a decrease in value. For example, when the index switched over from a 0.00 to a 1.00, this was an indication that VantagePoint was forecasting a change in market direction to the upside. Since the index

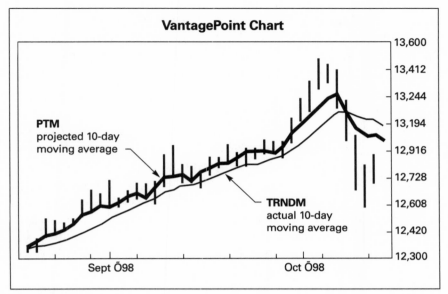

FIGURE 13-1.

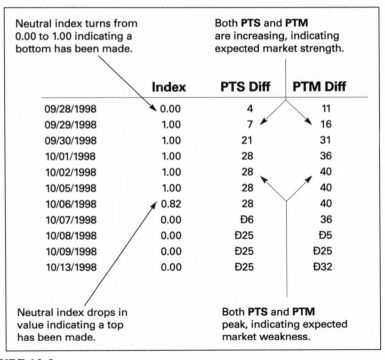

FIGURE 13-2.

is never more than 1.00, once it reaches 1.00 and remains there, VantagePoint expects the market to continue in an upward trend. You'll notice that from 10/05/98 to 10/06/98, there was a decrease from 1.00 to 0.82. Again, that indicates an expected turn in market direction, this time to the downside. It dropped further to a 0.00 and remained at 0.00 for several days, indicating a downward trend. The other two sections of the report go hand-in-hand. The PTS Diff is the difference between the actual 5-day moving average and a projected 5-day moving average that VantagePoint has predicted through its intermarket analysis capabilities. The PTM Diff is the difference between the actual 10-day moving average and a projected 10-day moving average. If the numbers in the PTS Diff and PTM Diff are positive and increasing, this indicates that VantagePoint expects the market to trend up. If the numbers are decreasing (they can even become negative numbers), this indicates an expected change in trend direction to the downside.

In these examples, you can see that when the Index was showing positive upward strength, the PTS Diff and PTM Diff were also showing positive upward strength. When the Index was showing weakness, the PTS Diff and PTM Diff were also showing weakness. When these three indicators are used in tandem with each other and are confirming each other, it increases the probability of a successful trade and gives the trader more confidence, since these indicators are independently derived through the use of several neural networks within VantagePoint.

In addition to the information above, VantagePoint predicts the next day's high and low to assist in identifying entry and exit points and help with setting stops. All of the information generated by VantagePoint is generated each day by taking into consideration intermarket relationships that exist between various selected markets and the forecasted market. This broadened context has allowed our clients to expand their technical analysis perspective to incorporate these intermarket dynamics.

Neal: Is there a Web site where readers can reach you?

Louis: Yes, it's www.profittaker.com.

Pit Stops

Barry Rudd's Trading Techniques

The following Chicago style trading technique is featured in my friend Barry Rudd's book on trading stocks. He originally developed this technique trading the futures market. This example shows a buy setup. Sell setups are the same, just inverted.

Dip and Rally

The trade described in Figure 13-3 is an intraday pattern of a 5-minute bar chart that is the basic "dip and rally" setup for a buy breakout.

You'll often see this pattern in equities. Obviously, this is an ideal, "textbook" example. But you would be surprised at the number of times you'll find this setup unfolding in the futures that you follow throughout each trading session.

Know where the price support and resistance areas are on a chart. These are areas that have halted the movement of a stock or commodity in the past. The more times a particular price has stalled the stock's movement, the stronger that support or resistance area becomes. Price support lines can be drawn horizontally through lows on a bar chart where price tended to bounce up. Price resistance lines can be drawn horizontally through

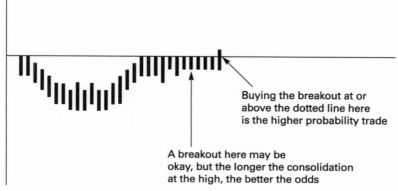

Buying the breakout at or above the dotted line here is the higher probability trade

A breakout here may be okay, but the longer the consolidation at the high, the better the odds

FIGURE 13-3.

highs on a chart. Very often, you will find that a support area will become a resistance area in the future. And likewise, a resistance area that a stock finally penetrates to the upside becomes a support area in the future.

The daily chart's support and resistance areas will help you better decide whether a trade setup is worth entering. If there is a lot of resistance just above where you buy, then you may want to pass up the trade. On the other hand, if a price resistance area is being broken or has recently broken through to the upside, a buy trade setup has a better chance of success. Look for these areas on the daily and intraday charts to find the nearest upside resistance level above the current price if you are buying or the next support level down if you are selling. Remember to not impose your ideas on the market. Instead, react to what it tells you with the daily and intraday setup patterns. The S/R levels will help you find the best trades to enter.

"Trading congestion" is something to stay away from. If a commodity or a stock is not trending, has narrow range daily bars (from high to low), or is just chopping sideways, then avoid it. Wait until it breaks out of congestion and begins some good daily price swing activity. This is when you look for the trade setups to act upon. Also, look at the recent average range of a daily price bar (from high to low). If that stock doesn't trade over a point or more on a regular basis, then you probably won't want to day-trade it. Look for the bigger profit opportunities with stocks that are currently in a "trader friendly" price swinging mode. For commodities, use 16 ticks for bonds and 10 cents for beans as a good average daily range.

You'll also notice that many times, the 50- and 200-day simple moving averages act as price support or resistance when trading equities. This is because many fund managers monitor these averages and use them in their buying and selling decisions. Being aware of where these lines are can aid your analysis. Support and resistance levels aid your decision-making for day-trades. They show *how far a commodity can be expected to move* up or down on both an intraday and daily time frame. This is the final step (or filter) to confirm a potential trade, or to rule it out.

Note: Barry's fax number is (214) 827-9530.

THOMAS R. PETERSON

Bullseye Trading Without the Arrows

Tom Peterson attended one of my seminars in California in November 1996. At that time, many forecasters in Chicago and on Wall Street were recommending going long the Canadian dollar, but he warned me not to get too bullish. It subsequently turned down and went into a significant swoon. Since then, we have been great phone pals. Tom trades for a living and consults to a select group of investors.

Neal: Your analysis is rather unusual in that it utilizes technical and fundamental analysis. How do you balance the two?

Tom: Since the first markets were traded, investment professionals have attempted using sophisticated analysis to try to understand trading relationships between price, volume, and time in an effort to gain an edge. Despite the fact that many great fortunes have been made by so-called "technical analysis" practitioners, it is still widely believed today—by uneducated investors—that technical analysis doesn't "work." That is to say that the prevailing propaganda maintains that investors cannot use technical analysis to consistently make money. If there is one style of analysis that works in most market environments, it is technical analysis, but technical analysis needs fundamental analysis in order to work properly. The best market traders have all been "tape readers" of one sort or another. That is because exceptional professional investors constantly look for evidence that their trading scenario is correct. They use a combination of fundamental analysis for the long-term overview and technical analysis for timing and confirmation of the fundamental outlook. If you are bullish on a particular investment, you need to see trading evidence that accumulation is predominating. If you are looking to sell, you need to see distribution evidence.

Neal: So how do you know when you are wrong?

Tom: Professionals know they are wrong when they start losing money. That sounds simplistic, but this is how professional traders approach trading. They keep their losses small, because they "scale" into positions. They look for their trades to behave as expected. And when they don't, they know that they have to at least step back and reassess their outlook. If a trader puts on a position and it doesn't immediately start to work in his favor, he knows that he is either wrong or early. He can't afford to impose his view of what the trade should do by sticking with or adding to a losing trade. Rigid thinkers thrive only in trending markets. Flexible thinkers make money in all markets, because they are willing to admit when they are wrong, if only temporarily. Being wrong is important information for the flexible thinker.

Neal: So, Tom, how do you plan to carry this message forward to the great masses of traders?

Tom: The Market Technicians Association has recently taken steps to try to earn increased investment industry respect. In July 1998, the Market Technicians Association was kind enough to publish an article I wrote wherein I advocated that technicians should not take it upon themselves to convert all the nonbelievers to the TA brand of analysis. I believe that it is proof enough for one to consistently make money, and that since TA provides an investor with a great tool, it is to one's advantage if only an educated minority practice it. I have even gone so far as to offer proof that using fundamental analysis *in isolation* doesn't "work." One need only pick up any daily newspaper to find sobering reports of fundamental analysts caught dead wrong and the subsequent plummet of a once-favored company's shares. In the real world of investing, one must constantly review one's holdings and look for signs that the investments are performing as they should.

Neal: Are you more oriented toward trading than toward long-term investing?

Tom: My preferred approach is to trade the short term with a portion of the portfolio. With the remainder, I prefer to invest for the intermediate term in sync with the trend, while using traditional asset allocation between stocks, debt instruments, and cash. I abhor the current fad of the so-called "buy and hold strategy." It really is a nonstrategy. You give up too many opportunities to lock in profits and sidestep risky markets with that approach. The credo of long-term investing is the refuge of the one-eyed analyst, who can only see bull markets and preaches the mantra of "buy and hold." This is the market equivalent of driving down the road, running over the detour signs, but driving straight ahead anyway in the belief that sooner or later, the road will get better. Along the way, the potholes may take out your tires and your car may get damaged, but you still drive blindly on, hoping (expecting) the rest of the convoy to follow you. Why wouldn't you take the detour and drive around the potholes? Because most drivers don't realize where they are on the map. They are too stubborn to back up when they find out they're in trouble, and besides, "in the long run," things always work out, assuming you haven't crashed in the meantime.

The financial markets, as everyone knows, have longer bull periods than bear periods. Whether your portfolio (or your nerve) survives the bear or a significant correction is a different matter. A balanced approach employing fundamental and technical analysis works best. Investors do not need to get too complex in their decision-making. The methods used for many decades still work the best.

Neal: Can you be more specific regarding why a simplified approach is better?

Tom: Much has been made about the failure of Long Term Capital Management (LTCM) and their particular brand of "rocket science," and rightly so. One of their lenders, UBS Bank, had to write off $700 million from LTCM losses and fired a bunch of senior executives responsible. That is just the tip of the iceberg, of course. The LTCM fiasco is very reminiscent of the Olympia and York debacle of the early 1990s. In both cases, it was deemed by bankers to be poor manners to ask the borrowing party to produce financial statements before lending (investing) huge amounts in their enterprises! Isn't it amazing how the banks make the same mistakes repeatedly? I think that this has something to do with the worship of academics in our culture. Studies with actual money in real-time (as opposed to simple back-testing) have shown that there is an inverse correlation between making money consistently in the market and the degree of complication in your investment approach. Many bankers, who have a passion for numbers, fall in love with the idea that if they just crunch the numbers enough, they can get an edge. This allows for increasingly complicated houses of cards like LTCM. They are based on a weak foundation. And by ignoring the technical evidence of increasing risk within the cycle, you can get these situations that can have a huge impact on the rest of the market—in fact, the rest of the world's markets.

Neal: You seem to be down on hedge funds.

Tom: Not at all. "Hedge Fund" in itself is a very broad term. The hedge fund approach that I like best, and the one I currently use in my own portfolio, is really a very aggressive approach that utilizes short-selling to make profits in overvalued situations and also trades the S&P to balance the short-term risk in the market.

On the other hand, there are hedge funds such as LTCM. As I understand it, hedge funds like LTCM try to capture the difference in spreads between debt instruments of different countries as one of their strategies. In my October 19, 1997, forecast, "Whistling Past the Graveyard" (which correctly anticipated the October 27 collapse), I mentioned that one technical indicator called the "Ted Spread" (the spread in interest rates between T-bills and Eurodollars) had widened to 95 points, and that normally a spread of 85 points would be a warning sign to the markets. Historically, the Ted Spread has been a measure of global risk, because Eurodollars are uninsured, whereas Treasury bills are very safe. Well, using this analogy, it stands to reason that since hedge funds are trying to capture what they think are inordinately wide spreads between issuers of different quality, they are doing what no professional trader should do, and therefore it is not surprising that they should get burned. Putting this another way, they were "fading" a warning sign! They were trying to put their market opinion above that of the market. This is a form of market arrogance, and usually, the practitioners of arrogance eventually have to learn humility.

Neal: So you see trading Chicago style as something that must evolve into a combination of technical and fundamental analysis?

Tom: Yes. I understand floor traders use this approach already. I believe that every trader would improve their performance if they were to adopt the Chicago-style approach that many floor "locals" use. With the proper application of technical tools, an intermediate-term investment approach will outperform every time, especially because avoiding market downdraft periods will allow the investor to maintain hard-earned profits from bull markets. Investing should be less like rocket science and more like golf: In the end, it doesn't matter how you get there; all that matters is how you score.

Neal: Tom, I am sure our readers appreciate your pragmatic approach.

Tom: Thank you.

Tom's e-mail address is trader8@home.com.

Pit Stops

THE BALLOONIST

A man is flying in a hot-air balloon and realizes he is lost. He reduces height and spots a man down below. He lowers the balloon further and shouts: "Excuse me, can you tell me where I am?"

The man below says, "Yes you're in a hot-air balloon, hovering 30 feet above this field."

"You must work in technical analysis," says the balloonist.

"I do," replies the man. "How did you know?"

"Well," says the balloonist, "everything you have told me is technically correct, but it's no use to anyone."

The man below says, "You must be a fundamental trader."

"I am," replies the balloonist, "but how did you know?"

"Well," says the man, "you don't know where you are or where you're going, but you expect me to be able to help. You're in the same position you were before we met, but now it's my fault."

And so it goes. Here in Chicago at least, we like to be technical traders until the next government report comes out.

MARK DOUGLAS

Minding Yourself Before the Trade

M ark Douglas is an author and trading coach. His book, *The Disciplined Trader,* is a must-read for any trader. Mark and I both attended Michigan State University. His clients include Chicago's top pit traders.

Neal: Mark, what is the most important skill a trader can develop?

Mark: The most fundamental skill a trader can acquire is the ability to truly accept the risks inherent in trading. The markets display collective behavior patterns that have statistically reliable outcomes. But the outcome of each individual pattern is probable. Winning is not assured; there is definitely a risk of losing money and being wrong.

The problem is that most traders erroneously assume that because they put on and take off trades, they must also be risktakers. For the vast majority of traders (in fact, all but the best), this couldn't be further from the truth. Yes, it is certainly true that trading is risky. And if you put on and take off a trade, you are also taking a risk. However, just because you trade doesn't mean that you have learned how to accept the risk in a way in which you can maintain a confident state of mind and at the same time remain disciplined and focused. There is a huge psychological gap between risk-taking and truly accepting the risk you are taking, with profound implications on the bottom line.

Neal: What does it mean to truly accept risk?

Mark: The best traders can admit they are wrong and take off a losing trader without the slightest bit of emotional discomfort. If you haven't yet learned the skill of risk acceptance, no trading system—technical, fundamental, or otherwise—will compensate for your susceptibility to the kinds of psychological errors mentioned above. When you think about it, or if you go back and review your trades, you'll most certainly find that it was the psychological errors that diminished your results, not your trading system or methodology. If you do this simple exercise and find this is the case, it will be a clear demonstration that more than anything else you could learn or do as a trader, your success is a function of your ability to maintain confidence, discipline, and focus.

Note: Mark Douglas may be reached at www.markdouglas.com.

Pit Stops

The Future of Trading Chicago Style

What is the future of trading Chicago style? I asked Larry Schulman. Larry is a former floor trader and assists traders in implementing strategies for the overseas markets. Larry is managing director of screen-based trading at Goldenberg, Hehmeyer & Co.

The two things that will make any exchange successful are market transparency (which includes access, price disclosure, and market information) and minimizing transaction costs (liquidity and direct costs). Electronic markets provide two things that market participants prefer. These are symmetry of information and equal access to market for all participants. However, both of these things are less important than transaction costs, in particular liquidity. Chicago traders are unsurpassed in providing liquidity anywhere in the world. The most stunning demonstration of this fact is the timing of the rapid switch of market share from LIFFE to DTB in the bund contract in late 1997. The shift of market share occurred simultaneously with DTB allowing remote memberships from Chicago. This brilliant marketing decision allowed DTB to get Chicago locals to compete with LIFFE locals in providing liquidity for the contract. On the surface what is a triumph for electronic trading over open outcry is in reality a ringing endorsement of the skills of Chicago traders.

What does this mean for floor trading and open outcry versus electronic trading? Electronic trading permits exceptional traders to trade in several pits simultaneously and participate on equal footing with a local trader who stands next to the biggest brokers. Electronic trading should eventually supplant open outcry: The superior traders will realize that they will make more money at the expense of mediocre traders because fewer traders will be required to provide the liquidity to attract market participants. In addition, electronic trading removes barriers to entry that make the most liquid pits natural monopolies. In established, liquid markets, new traders have a great deal of trouble trading with brokers and becoming visible to other market participants. The added amount of time to acquire the skills necessary to be a successful market maker makes the entry cost prohibitive to most participants. Electronic trading allows new participants the opportunity to trade on an equal footing to the most established traders, and it greatly reduces the cost of entry into the markets, thus ensuring a constant flow of new talent and capital into the market that would otherwise find its way into other businesses.

More than anything else, the changing technological landscape and shifting market shares have demonstrated the superiority of Chicago market makers. It points out the importance of trading skill in creating liquid markets and will ultimately create an environment where risk management skills born in the pits can be exported throughout the world without leaving the shores of Lake Michigan or missing a single Bulls game.

Note: Larry Schulman may be reached at Goldenberg-Hehmeyer, (312) 922-6765.

Pit Stops

NOTES FROM AN AT-HOME DAY-TRADER

Earl is a cyberspace pal I met on a newsgroup list.

Neal: Tell me about your day-trading in the Chicago markets.

Earl: I spend six and a half hours a day, four days a week trading an average of two to three times per day, although some days I'll go without any trades at all. For prep, I spend an hour before markets open, a couple of hours in the evening, and six hours or so on weekends, in total, about 45 hours per week. My trades are generally of short duration, 5 to 10 minutes or less for losers and under 60 minutes for winners. There are periods during the day, particularly from 10 to 12 o'clock (mountain time), when I set alarms on my charts and do other things, including e-mail, reading, and systems development. Sometimes I just walk out on my deck and take a break. I have no compulsion for action, and I never, ever take a trade I don't like.

My trading is performed entirely on-line in small lots using relatively light leverage, i.e., nowhere near exchange minimums.

Looking over October, 60 percent of my trades have been losers, the majority at 0 to 0.5 points, none more than 2 points. However, the other 40 percent allowed me to exceed my monthly day-trade point budget by the middle of last week. Throw in a couple of good position trades and it's already been a very nice month. It took many years of failure, study, and preparation to get here, and I've still got a lot to learn. Most would-be traders don't make it because they run out of trading capital for lack of sound money management; they run out of living capital for lack of time to learn to trade; or they never acquire the required psychological capital.

ANDREW SCHUMACHER

How the Institutions Trade

Andrew and I first met when we did consulting together for a bank in Warsaw: not Warsaw, Indiana—Warsaw, Poland.

Commerz Futures L.L.C. specializes in offering technology-enhanced services in exchange-traded derivatives to institutional and high net worth client accounts. As a wholly owned subsidiary of Commerzbank AG, one of Germany's leading financial institutions, Commerz provides access to all major futures and options exchanges worldwide, offering execution and clearing services, facilities management operations, managed funds, and a state-of-the-art 24-hour electronic market order desk.

Neal: What is your position at Commerzbank?

Andy: Vice president, Global Futures Trading at Commerz Futures L.L.C., a wholly owned subsidiary of Commerzbank AG. My chief responsibility is our 24-hour electronic trading desk for institutional futures and options clients. Equipped with Eurex trader workstations, Matif/Monep GL/NSC terminals, CME GLOBEX2 and CBOT Project A workstations, and NYMEX ACCESS terminals, we provide execution services for our international clients via electronic trading terminals and order-routing systems. We also provide complete service to the worldwide open-outcry exchanges, either directly or through intermediaries.

Neal: Andy, when I mention trading Chicago style, what comes to mind? What do you think it will evolve into?

Andy: Certainly the first things that come to mind when you mention trading Chicago style are the massive S&P and Eurodollar pits at the CME and the airport hangar–like financial pit at the CBOT. These markets are like no other in the world. It is impossible for the uninitiated not to be awed by the sheer spectacle and physical nature of any one of these markets during active trading hours. Up until very recently, the open-outcry pit-trading style of the CBOT and the CME and the membership structure of the exchanges themselves have provided the model for how to transact futures business.

But now, the markets that are still open-outcry–based, such as Chicago, have seen their membership seat prices plummet. The current three-pronged strategy is to use electronic trading outside traditional pit hours, provide both methods of order execution during the day, and in some cases develop partnerships with European and Asian markets to route electronic orders to the existing trading floors. But as these exchanges pour resources into supporting each of these initiatives and allow time for membership voting in order to approve actions, the new electronic exchanges are gaining experience and market share. The proliferation of electronic exchanges, the growth in electronic trading volumes on mainly open-outcry exchanges, as well as recent or planned transitions from open-outcry to screen-based systems at the Matif, LIFFE, and SFE have proven that the new business model of an electronic trading environment managed by a for-profit corporate structure will be the model as we go forward.

Chicago, like most other financial centers, is currently in a transition phase. The rise in Internet order-routing systems and electronic trading terminals has forced many market participants, such as local floor traders, CTAs, and brokerage houses, to forever alter the way they conduct business. Imagine a world where the floor trader, trading at an electronic terminal, can't "sense" the mood of the market by seeing the confusion in the eyes of his neighbors or hearing the panic in their voices? How does a technical CTA, who has always used daily open and closing signals to make his trading decisions, operate when the markets trade virtually around the clock? How does a Futures Commission Merchant (FCM) keep a 24-hour trading desk staffed with experienced operators capable of executing orders via electronic terminals, order-routing software and open-outcry pits in over 300 futures and options contracts worldwide? Three major changes will occur. More locals will adapt to electronic trading or leave the marketplace. The markets they trade and the hours they keep will no longer be set in stone. They will have to find new ways to gain an "edge" in the market. Brokerage houses and exchanges as well as all the supporting players, such as software and data vendors, will adapt their business models to support this. Central common meeting places will decrease in size, while upstairs electronic trading rooms will expand. Many brokerage firms are already providing traders with the facilities to trade the international markets via a PC rather than putting them on one of the exchange floors. The demand for this is growing as new generations of computer-literate traders are more comfortable with electronic order placement.

Neal: What does this mean for retail customers?

Andy: Retail customers must harness this newfound flood of information and power. Traders will have access to information from an array of sources. The brokers will give less advice and information but provide more interpretation of information and assume more risk and technology management. The exchange-broker-trader relationship will change as exchanges look to access the customers more directly, rather than relying on the brokerage houses. This will cause them to rethink their role and will lead to the growth of third-party software providers as end-users demand easier, more transferable interfaces, rather than learning the various intricacies of each individual system. The number of major exchanges and clearing FCMs will decline as per-trade profits continue to decrease and the cost of starting and supporting the technology infrastructure increases. The futures and options product will be wrapped into the product mix of the global-bank–owned FCM capable of spreading these costs over a larger client base. Exchanges that have already seen the speed and cost savings of bringing new products to market electronically, but also have experienced the financial expense and expertise needed to upgrade and maintain vast computer networks, will continue to merge and partner with other exchanges. The number of smaller, specialized Internet or electronic exchanges designed to handle specific markets may grow because of low barriers to entry. This will also force major exchanges to adapt to meet the threat.

As always, the individuals and firms that learn from their own mistakes and the mistakes of others and react to these changes fastest and most efficiently will be able to reap the benefits. Those that don't will lose money, market share, and their livelihood.

Neal: What mistakes have you seen traders make?

Andy: The mistakes have been documented in countless books on the subject. Some of the more common mistakes I have seen include the following, not necessarily in order of importance:

1. *Trading on emotions.* I call it the "I'm right, but the market is wrong" syndrome. You hear traders say things like "Boy, I really called this market right today" or "Man, I read this market all wrong." The human need to be "right" clouds rational thought as to what the appropriate action might be in a quickly changing set of circumstances. A corollary to this in technical traders would be "My system just doesn't trade well in this type of market." The best traders, who make profits over the long term, take as much emotion out of trading as possible, regardless of dollar value. They liquidate when they are incorrect. When they have a profitable trade, they are just as curious about why the trade is profitable as for unprofitable trades. They are cautiously optimistic when the market is moving in the direction they intended, and they exit the trade either by a preset strategy or when the set of circumstances under which they entered the trade are no longer present. They see it as more of a strategy exercise, with constantly changing variables or trade market structure imbalances that have the best risk-reward ratio. They do not make money every time or even the majority of the time, but their losers are smaller and their winners are bigger.

2. *Thinking that things won't change.* Another big mistake is perceiving a string of winning trades as proof of their trading prowess and failing to recognize that the set of circumstances in the marketplace that made these trades winners is temporary and can change overnight. They may have gotten lucky, or they may have understood briefly the forces affecting the market and anticipated movements correctly, but it was just that . . . briefly.

3. The third mistake is *overtrading*. This can mean both the need to always have a position on, regardless of whether the trader's criteria are met, and entering and exiting trades without a valid reason.

4. *Lack of discipline.* Countless intelligent traders trade successfully for a very extended period of time only to lose it all on one trade or one very short, defined period of market turmoil. I've seen it happen to some of the smallest individual traders and the largest money managers in the world. The ability to adopt and adhere to a rigid, per-trade risk limit can be difficult for all traders.

5. A fifth mistake is the *inability of traders to adapt* to either a substantial increase or decrease in funds. The trader who has the enviable problem of a sudden increase in account size often fails to realize that his particular trading system or the market that he trades may not be as suited to the larger positions that he will be managing. A 10-lot market on-close order in the soybean oil futures contract will have a greatly different impact on the market than a 500-lot order.

Neal: Would you say most of your traders are system-technical or discretionary traders?

Andy: Certainly there are some of both. The trend is toward system-technical. Most of the global banks have decreased their appetite for proprietary trading risk in general as they try to smooth out erratic returns to the bottom line. This fits better with traders who can clearly define their parameters and show viable, consistent track records. I find that discretionary traders also seem to have a harder time as information is more available to a wider audience at the same time and traditional sources of market information have changed. I am not commenting on who makes more money or who is the better trader. If you look at the top traders, their funds under management, and their long-term returns, you won't find many that trade by the seat of their pants. Most of them utilize complex, multilayered trading engines that were already revolutionary at their inception and have been constantly updated to adapt to both changing market conditions and the desired risk-reward ratio of their intended investor.

Neal: Can you describe some of the similarities or differences between "good" traders and "bad" traders?

Andy: This may sound strange, but all the long-term successful traders that I have been in contact with knew everything about the products they were trading. I mean everything: from underlying deliverables, expiration dates, and historical spread differentials during volatile markets to who the major players are and how opening prices are calculated. They use this information to their advantage. Unsuccessful traders say things like "As long as I can see the prices and get a chart, I can trade it." This isn't trading. This is gambling. The successful traders I have dealt with are not trying to reinvent the wheel, pick the top or bottom of the market, or look for the latest trading system. They take a disciplined, proven approach, start small, and learn from their mistakes.

Neal: Do you believe in the back-testing of trading systems?

Andy: I'll give you what sounds like a politically correct answer: yes and no. All successful traders do some amount of testing in a simulated environment before going "live" where they are actually losing or making money. But they also understand that real-world trading can and will have different results. I have also seen traders with Ph.D.s in astrophysics who have back-tested their systems for years but were baffled when their system went haywire when they had real money in their account and had to place actual trades in the markets. They didn't bother to learn the details of markets, such as active trading months, liquidity, bid-ask spread norms, and stop slippage.

Neal: What type of capitalization do you require of customers?

Andy: Commerz Futures is restricted to clearing institutional clients by the definition of the Federal Reserve. Our clients are mostly proprietary traders or treasury people who work for international financial institutions. We also execute orders for the customers of other institutions that clear their customers' accounts but don't handle all the execution services.

Neal: What are some of the new or less-known exchange-traded financial derivative products that you or your traders deal with on a daily basis, and how would they impact Chicago-style trading?

Andy: Successful futures traders quickly realize that their trading style may suit many different markets. Information on new products is now available free of charge from most exchange Web sites. In the past, if a trader asked a broker about a new product that the broker either didn't understand or didn't know about, the broker would usually try to dissuade the client from using this product. Now, the business gravitates to the firms that have the most expertise in certain product areas, where knowledgeable brokers can advise traders on the nuances of trading those products and provide the best service. This has the effect of shortening the business cycle. Information is disseminated more quickly. Instead of having to build physical trading pits and the physical infrastructure to support them, exchanges find out faster if a new product is a hit or miss.

The products we deal with that are less-known is really just a question of the level of sophistication and geographic location. Since we are a subsidiary of a global European bank headquartered in Chicago, we spend a great deal of time educating U.S. clients about European financial products. This includes larger exchanges, such as the LIFFE, EUREX and Matif, as well as smaller exchanges, such as the new Hanover Exchange and exchanges in Spain and Italy. In the last several months, we have become experts in Euro-conversion operations in the futures markets. We also end up acting as a Chicago futures market specialist to European, Latin American, and Pacific Rim clients. For example, January 3 was the first time you could trade the new Euro-FX futures on the CME's GLOBEX2 system. Everyone wanted to know the contract size, pricing convention, settlement process, and bid-ask spread. Our business is mainly centered around financial products. Traders want liquidity, speed of execution, low cost, and readily available news regarding the products. Products such as major debt instruments and stock-index futures contracts generally fall into this category. German Bunds, French Nationals, Nikkei futures, and Euromarks are a few that come to mind. Certain commodity trading advisors may only be interested in a product that trends well or has enough historical price data to meet the criteria of their trading system regardless of volume or open interest. So although a technical trader doesn't understand the fundamentals behind the three-month Euribor contract, dried red aduki beans, and the MSCI Taiwan Stock Index futures, they may work very well with his trading system. The fund managers that we deal with are using any product that fits into their portfolio mix. This could mean anything from CME Eurodollar futures to the TSE JGB futures contract. So Chicago style can exist, but not always Chicago products.

Neal: Andy, some people would say you have the dream job. Do you agree?

Andy: No. I think most people in the financial markets who are reading this book consider sitting on their yachts trading their own accounts and not really having to worry about whether they have a losing or winning month to be the ultimate dream job.

My responsibility is handling client business. If you are looking for set hours and job security or you don't like fast-paced change and confrontation, it's not the place for you. Most of the time you are managing chaos. If the markets aren't going through volatile swings, then the exchanges are changing their software, someone just launched a new contract, your largest client wants to leave because he is unhappy with his fill, or you're worried about the staffing on the third shift. Basically, from Sunday afternoon at 3:00 p.m. CST to Friday at 4:00 p.m. CST, you're on call, anytime, day or night. At the same time, the industry is still consolidating, and profit margins are continuing to decline. If you're talking about exchange-traded futures and options, this is the direction the business is heading, and I'd rather be on the leading edge than the lagging end. In the 1980s there was tremendous growth in the use of the international futures markets by traders. So far, in the 1990s electronic trading terminals have had a great impact on the way traders access the markets. Now, third-party software providers are on the leading edge, supplying traders with common, front-end user devices designed to interface with the open architecture data feeds from the exchanges that enable them to access multiple exchanges at the same time from one screen. Through all these developments, one thing hasn't changed. Whether it's Frankfurt-style, Tokyo-style, or Chicago-style, good traders are *still* hard to find.

Neal: One final question.

Andy: Okay.

Neal: Next time we fly to Poland, can I have the window seat?

Andy: No!

Andy is currently employed at Warburg, Dillon, and Read. He can be reached at (312) 554-6610.

Pit Stops

You Make the Call

You feel you are trading or that your system is smarter than the market. Keep this story in mind.

CANADIANS: Please divert your course 15 degrees to the south to avoid a collision.

AMERICANS: Recommend you divert your course 15 degrees to the north to avoid a collision.

CANADIANS: Negative. You will have to divert your course 15 degrees to the south to avoid a collision.

AMERICANS: This is the captain of a U.S. Navy ship. I say again, divert *your* course.

CANADIANS: No. I say again, divert *your* course.

AMERICANS: This is the aircraft carrier *U.S.S. Lincoln*, the second-largest ship in the United States' Atlantic Fleet. We are accompanied by three destroyers, three cruisers, and numerous support vessels. I demand that you change your course 15 degrees north—I say again, that's one-five degrees north—or countermeasures will be undertaken to ensure the safety of this ship. We are on a military mission and we will take any and all measures to ensure the integrity of this mission. Do you understand?

CANADIANS: This is a lighthouse. Your call.

CHUCK LEBEAU

Looking for the Fire Exit or Fire Wall

The Internet and newsgroups are important in terms of getting ideas for trading from a fundamental or technical analysis viewpoint. The following exchanges were in response to two questions I asked, over the Net, of my friend Chuck LeBeau. Chuck has lectured at both my Chicago and L.A. seminars.

Neal: Chuck, any ideas for placing stops when trading Chicago markets?

Chuck: Well, one is the Chandelier Exit. We have often advocated the importance of good exits and this is one of my favorites. The exit stop is placed at a multiple of average true ranges from the highest high or highest close since the entry of the trade. As the highs get higher, the stop moves up, but it never moves downward. (*Note:* Average true range is the actual range, taking into account gaps caused by reports, fast markets, etc.)

Examples:

Exit at the highest high since entry minus 3 ATR on a stop.

Exit at the highest close since entry minus 2.5 ATR on a stop.

Application: We like the Chandelier Exit as one of our exits for trend-following systems. (The name is derived from the fact that the exit is hung downward from the ceiling of a market.)

This exit is extremely effective at letting profits run in the direction of a trend while still offering some protection against a major reversal in trend. In fact, our research has shown that this exit is so effective that you can enter futures markets at random, and if you use this exit, the results over time will be profitable. (If you don't believe us, just try it.) When used for long-term trend following, the best values for the ATR in most markets range somewhere between 2.5 and 4.0.

Neal: You also have another exit.

Chuck: Yes, the Yo-Yo Exit. This exit is very similar to the Chandelier Exit except that the ATR stop is always pegged to the most recent close instead of the highest high. Since the closes move higher and lower, the stop also moves up and down (hence the yo-yo name). Although this stop appears similar to the Chandelier Exit, the logic is quite a bit different. The Yo-Yo Exit is a classic volatility stop that is intended to recognize an abnormal adverse price fluctuation that occurs in one day. This abnormal volatility is often the result of a news event or some important technical reversal that is likely to signal the end of a trend. This logic makes the Yo-Yo Exit very effective, and we seldom regret being stopped-out whenever this exit is triggered.

We should caution you that the Yo-Yo Exit should never be your only loss protection, because if the price moves slowly against your position, the Yo-Yo Exit also moves away each day, and in theory, the stop may never be hit.

The Yo-Yo and the Chandelier exits work best when used together. The Chandelier Exit is typically set at 3 ATRs or more from a high point and never lowered; therefore, it will protect against any gradual reversal of trend. The Yo-Yo Exit is typically set at only 1.5 to 2.0 ATRs from the most recent close and will protect our position from unusual one-day spikes in volatility. When used together, the operative stop each day would be whichever of the two stops is closest.

Neal: Do you couple this with money management advice?

Chuck: When using any stops based on multiples of ATR, we should keep in mind that volatility can quickly expand to where our risk isn't greater than we intended. We do not want to unknowingly exceed the risk limitations dictated by our money management scheme, so we should also have a "worst case" dollar-based stop available or be prepared to reduce our position size quickly as the ATR values expand. When should we reduce our position size and when should we implement our fixed-dollar stop?

If we are on the right side of the volatility expansion, it may not be wise to reduce our position size just as the trade is beginning to do what we hoped for. For this reason, I prefer to implement the dollar-based stop on profitable positions, rather than reducing the size of winning positions prematurely. We obviously want to have big positions in our winners and small positions in our losers. Therefore, it would make sense to reduce our position size only if the volatility is increasing in a trade that is going against us.

Once extremely large profits have been achieved, positions can safely be reduced without sacrificing too much in the way of potential profits.

Neal: Thanks Chuck.

Chuck LeBeau's e-mail address is chuck@traderclub.com.

Pit Stops

Employment

General Description. Employment is the single most important economic data series for the financial markets because it is an extremely timely and comprehensive measure of business activity. As such, this report is always a major focus of politicians and monetary policy officials and, in turn, commands the full attention of the financial markets around the world. Generally, employment is viewed as one of the best concurrent measures of business activity, although some studies have shown that employment lags output changes.

Economic Indicator Information at a Glance—Employment

Market significance	Very high
Typical release time	8:30 a.m. Eastern Time; first Friday of the month
Released by	Labor Department Bureau of Labor Statistics
Period covered	Prior month
Web site	http://statts.bls.gov:80/newsrels.htm

On the day that the employment report is released, the commissioner of the Bureau of Labor Statistics has a monthly briefing on the employment situation for members of the Joint Economic Committee of Congress. At that hearing, the commissioner reviews, amplifies, and qualifies the employment data and discusses any known anomalies in or forthcoming changes to the data. When Congress is not in session, the commissioner holds a press conference to discuss the report.

Because the employment report has so many complex dimensions, at times financial market participants tend to dissect this report more than most economic reports. Moreover, in recent years, the financial markets tend to be more susceptible to mundane technical issues associated with the employment report methodology. Consequently, the level of technical detail included in the following discussion is intentionally far greater than in other chapters.

Understanding the Data.   The U.S. Labor Department's Bureau of Labor Statistics (BLS) produces two independently derived measures of employment on a monthly basis. The *establishment,* or *payroll,* measure is based on payroll records and measures employment in nonagricultural industries. The second measure, *household employment,* is based on a survey and measures civilian, noninstitutional employment of persons aged 16 years and older and includes agricultural workers and self-employed individuals.

This information is adapted from *Trading the Fundamentals,* Revised Edition, by Michael P. Niemira and Gerald F. Zukowski; 1998, The McGraw-Hill Companies, Inc.

THE COMMITTEE

REAL TRADES, REAL-TIME, NO GURUS ALLOWED

The following interview is a composite of traders outside the Chicago area who trade the Chicago markets.

One of the members of the committee reminded me that his grandfather started as a runner at the Board of Trade in the 1920s and retired as senior vice-president of a major brokerage house.

Since it is clear that systems and the computer will dominate Chicago-style trading in the years ahead, how these people view that and other developments in the Chicago markets should prove both informative and interesting. The members of the committee asked not to be identified for twelve months following the publication of this book.

Neal: Let's start with the youngest member of the committee. You have spent much time and effort meeting and teaching traders. You must have a unique perspective on traders?

Committee: Two years ago, I toured the country leading seminars on how to use TradeStation by Omega Research. During that time, I met approximately 600 investors.

Neal: How many of those investors told you they were successful with the systems they used in the past?

Committee: Only three, but all 600 hoped to be successful system traders. Of the three, one bought a system and the other two developed their own. One spent four years developing his system and the other, six years. The one characteristic they both shared was their determination to study the markets and all materials available on systems development. Ultimately, they both wondered why it took them so long to discover the simplicity of their systems. This reminds me of an old quote, "Facts are a lot like cows: they disappear the longer you stare at them."

Neal: What do cows have to do with markets and systems?

Committee: This means that the more you study the markets and systems, the more likely you will eventually get beyond the surface and find the interrelationships within the markets. This is what happens in the cow analogy. After studying the cows, you see their environment and all the interrelationships between the cows and their environment. It can take a long time to get beneath the surface to discover the important relationships. And after a while you do not see the cows; you see the relationships.

Neal: Relationships, we always come back to that point. Let me ask the entire committee: Are you all big believers in systems?

Committee: Over these past 20 years, we have gone from one extreme to the other. There were times when we felt like systems could do everything and other times we felt systems could do nothing. We *can* say that there are not many good systems out there for the investor. It is easier for a software developer to write a good press release than produce a good system.

Neal: Why is that?

Committee: The implication is that if you design a great system, then why sell it? Why not use it to manage money? We have never found a good answer for that. Perhaps the developer doesn't have the temperament to trade, or maybe he likes getting an income without risking any of his capital. Now, we don't want to paint all developers with the same brush and say they market substandard systems. What we are saying is that there are good systems out there, but there are not many of them.

Neal: Does everyone have a system? Let me ask one committee member to answer.

Committee: Yes, everyone has a system, whether it is written or internalized. I refer to an internalized system as intuition. In both types of systems, there are rules to follow. I prefer a mechanical system because it forces a decision. There is no emotion or second-guessing involved. I require myself to make the trade, with no backing out.

Neal: Is a mechanical system better than a discretionary system?

Committee: Not necessarily. A system is a decision-making model consisting of rules. The rules are followed and a decision is made. A mechanical or discretionary system does not affect the quality of the model and its underlying rules. The decision-making rules are of primary importance. A limitation of discretionary trading is the small number of markets followed. Someone has to watch the markets if it's discretionary. An individual can watch only so many markets. Many times, the discretionary trader concentrates on one market. A mechanical system can be used on all markets. I've found trading in fewer markets leads to uneven returns. Some months are profitable and others are not. Trading many markets tends to smooth this out.

Neal: Not everyone is a system developer. What criteria do you suggest an individual use to evaluate a system? Let me ask the elder statesman of the committee to answer.

Committee: There are numerous ways to evaluate a system. The two that I found most helpful to the individual investor are the Maximum Drawdown and the Sharpe Ratio. Maximum Drawdown is the maximum total dollars lost from the highest high of your profits to the lowest low. This is important to the investor because if he trades and goes into a drawdown, then all kinds of things can happen. As you go into a drawdown, feelings of anxiety increase and the resultant actions can be catastrophic. The investor can continue trading, stop trading, or modify his system. The last two usually work against him. A good system will weather the drawdown just fine. It is the investor who may not do so well. This is why I like Maximum Drawdown. Drawdowns happen to everyone. The question then arises regarding what to do about drawdown? Before buying a system, the investor needs to ask, "How much money can I afford to lose before my anxiety level rises to such a point that it makes me an ineffective trader?" I personally have a low threshold for anxiety. Therefore, I have set 10% as the maximum drawdown I can tolerate.

Neal: Many systems have maximum drawdowns greater than 10%. Is there anything you sacrifice by having a smaller drawdown? Let me direct this question to the member of the committee who trades a fund.

Committee: Yes, I sacrifice my rate of return. There are some systems that might offer a higher rate of return, but the drawdowns are usually greater. This is where individuals have to make their own decisions. If you can handle a 30% to 60% drawdown in order to get a higher rate of return, then more power to you.

Neal: Tell me about the Sharpe Ratio.

Committee: The Sharpe Ratio shows the variability of your rate of return. There is a lot in the literature about better formulas, but the Sharpe Ratio is used everywhere. I find it to be a good starting point in system evaluation. A high Sharpe Ratio is good and implies low variability, while a low Sharpe Ratio implies high variability.

Neal: Does a high Sharpe Ratio result in a high rate of return?

Committee: No, only the variability of the rate of return is measured. Let me give you some examples. Let's assume you have a system with a 36% rate of return. If this system made 3% every month, then the Sharpe Ratio would be high. If this system gained 10% one month and lost 7% the next, and all the following months had these big swings, the result would be a low Sharpe Ratio. Now let's try another system that has a 12% rate of return. If the system made 1% per month, then the Sharpe Ratio would be high. If the monthly return was up 6% one month, down 7% the next, and continued on with such great variability, the result would be a low Sharpe Ratio. So a high Sharpe Ratio is important for someone who doesn't want a lot of variability in his or her system, who wants a steady rate of return on a month-to-month basis.

Neal: What is your cutoff point for a Sharpe Ratio?

Committee: I've heard it said that if a CTA (commodity trading advisor) wants to stay in business, then a Sharpe Ratio of 0.7 or higher is needed. This applies to the individual investor. If the investor wants to stay in business and continue trading, then his system needs a Sharpe Ratio higher than 0.7.

As I stated earlier, there are other great criteria for evaluating systems, but these two hit the investor right where he's at.

The individual investor will stop trading at the point that he loses a certain amount of money from his account. If the individual can use a system that matches or exceeds my criteria above, he will continue trading for a long time.

Neal: Let me ask the statistical guru of the group what statistical tools he uses to trade.

Committee: When I first started developing trading systems, I began with regression analysis. This analysis was developed back in the latter part of the 19th century. The purpose of regression analysis is to develop a multivariable predictive equation. I used Stepwise Regression. This analyzed all the variables I supplied, chose the best one, and then went on to choose the second best, and so on. This analysis would choose only the worthwhile variables and leave out the "garbage" variables. I began with 60 variables, and the resulting formulas usually contained anywhere from two to ten variables. After this, I graduated to Genetic Algorithms to test different variables. I usually tested several hundred variables. I was continuously looking for good variables to use in market prediction.

Neal: How did your early efforts turn out?

Committee: The results were mediocre. There were two reasons for this. First, with all the variables I tested, both the regression analysis and the genetic algorithm assumed a linear relationship. By linear, I mean "cause and effect." For example, I assumed that if a variable rose 20%, then the commodity's price would rise by 10%. However, this did not happen. I didn't find a meaningful cause-and-effect relationship. I am not denying the existence of a cause-and-effect relationship in the markets. I am only saying that in my early days, I did not find a good predictive variable or combination of variables. The second reason involves a danger that can affect all of us today, "curve fitting." Every writer of systems has to address curve fitting because it can easily occur. My definition of curve fitting is taking historical data and analyzing it to produce a system that looks great historically but has so many variables that it is untradeable in real time. The mistake is adding another rule (variable) to handle an exception so the historical trading looks fantastic.

Neal: How do you avoid curve fitting?

Committee: From my own studies, I have come to agree with the literature. It states that five or fewer variables will likely avoid curve fitting. I am very comfortable with three variables. Having four variables makes me slightly uneasy. And a system with five variables is to be closely watched. Using six or more variables is dangerous. One reservation I have about neural nets arises over the issue of curve fitting. A neural net can examine hundreds of variables and put them together in untold combinations. This leads to another question I was often asked during my seminars. How many trades should I have on a historical test before I consider the results statistically reliable? According to sampling theory, the answer is 30 or more (closed) trades. I developed a long-term system that had only seven trades, and six were winners. Someone else asked me if I would trade a system that looked good but had fewer than 30 trades in its historical testing. This is a matter of personal preference. I would trade the system, but I would not risk much of my capital on it.

Neal: Do you optimize your systems?

Committee: I used to optimize everything I could. I found the historic results were great and real-time trading results were not. I am not against optimization, but now I use it very sparingly. During one of my past studies, I wanted to optimize variables every day and then see if I could make money by trading the next day. It didn't work. I believe the reason it didn't was the variables I used back then. This is important because it showed me there might be a world of indicators out there, but very few could explain the market's actions. If I encounter a good predictive variable, then I optimize it initially and I don't bother with it any further.

Neal: So what is your opinion of systems that optimize periodically?

Committee: Generally, they are low on my list of systems I want to work with. It reminds me of going for medical treatment and only having your symptoms treated. The root cause of the problem is not addressed, and new symptoms show up that need treating again. I believe a system that needs periodic optimization does not contain good explanatory variables. The optimization treats a surface phenomenon but does not get to the root cause of what makes the market move.

Neal: What other statistical methods do you use?

Committee: One of my favorites is *factor analysis*. Factor analysis is defined as an analysis technique to reduce a large number of variables to a more manageable set of dimensions or underlying constructs which explain a large portion of the variability among the various measures. In plain English, factor analysis is used to group commodities together by profits. Each single group contains a number of highly correlated commodities. I am a great believer in portfolio diversification and I use factor analysis to check how well I've diversified. Here is an example of how I check my portfolio's diversification. Let's say I want to develop a portfolio using 90 different commodities. First, I run all the commodities through my system, using a ten-year period. The results I use are the daily change in equity for each commodity. The result is 90 columns, each containing the daily equity change. The rows all line up according to date. Now I run the factor analysis on the data. If the result is 30 groups, then I am very happy. This means there are 30 groupings that are not correlated to each other. Also, one group has a very small effect on my total portfolio. If the result was three groupings, then I would be very concerned. If one of those three groups sustained major losses, then this would prove disastrous.

Factor analysis provides another benefit for investors interested in spreads. Within each group there are a number of highly correlated commodities. For example, one group may contain grains, another European currencies, and so forth. I found the commodities within a group, although highly correlated, have a spread that widens and narrows. If an investor wants to trade spreads, then factor analysis can identify potential spreads. Any single group contains a number of commodities with the potential for spread trading.

Neal: Concerning risk: Why is it the average investor doesn't understand that the more money he puts into the markets, the more money he can lose? This question is directed to the entire committee and I will write a composite answer.

Committee: The speculators' driving need for a system is their attempt to control risk. Pyramiding profits is the way to financial oblivion. Many speculators don't understand regression to the mean. The speculator starts out with some wins and then hubris kicks in. They put in more trades with higher risk and then they're hit with major losses. Chicago traders understand regression to the mean, and they know that in the long run, speculators will lose. Regression to the mean applies to everyone. Look at this year's hot superstars; their overall long-term performance will be average.

Let me expand a little more on risk. Neal, as you've stated, "Everyone spends his whole life trying to control risk, but there is always a torpedo with your name on it, aimed right at you." A speculator can go to seminars and listen to gurus say, "You can make a lot of money with little risk." Don't believe it. Look at the performance of stock managers versus the stock indices. Most underperform the market. If professional money managers have a hard time beating the market, then how can the speculator beat the professional traders in Chicago? It's not likely to happen.

Speculators must look at risk in terms of probability. What will happen if the worst case scenario occurs? Plan every trade with the worst case scenario in mind. This means you do not increase your risk as your account size increases.

Neal: You are so right on this. Trading Chicago style is being risk averse. We may not all understand all the systems, but we do have a feeling for risk. I am amazed by people attending seminars given by someone who got lucky and then markets it as the holy grail. For the techies reading this book, I have an additional question: What is your opinion of the new Java-based programs on the Internet?

Committee: These are exciting times coming our way. The Internet has opened up a whole new paradigm for the investor. There is a lot of Internet trading now, but the new Internet paradigm will bring the following changes:

The distribution channel, from the system developer to the investor, will change. In the future you will see systems accessed and used in cyberspace. Instead of downloading a program onto your computer, it will stay out on the Internet. You will access and use it out in cyberspace. This will more than likely mean an entirely new cost structure. Instead of paying $1000 to $2000 for a program that may or may not be workable, the trader of the future will pay a monthly fee. The monthly fee will be short-term instead of a long-time period. Another variation will be to use software programs for free. In order to support themselves, providers will sell advertising on their Web site. Imagine software that costs thousands of dollars now available for free in the near future.

You will choose your data provider in cyberspace. No special equipment, such as radio or satellite receivers, is necessary. All you will need is access to the Internet.

The Internet will place trades automatically for the trader. I remember when S&P traders were so excited because they could stay at home and with one click of the button fill their orders in 10 seconds. Many were looking to automate the placing of trades. Clicking the button will be outmoded.

Neal: How is this going to work?

Committee: The small investor will use a provider of these integrated services. First, you are given a choice of the various on-line data providers. The next two choices are what commodities to trade and which systems to use. If unsure, then you can do historical testing of each system. Therefore, the startup costs and potential early trading losses will be minimized.

Neal: What happens if it doesn't work?

Committee: The beauty of future Internet trading will be the option of paper trading. Can you imagine that? After you sign up, then let it run for a month or two and watch the results on paper. Instead of spending hundreds or thousands of dollars on systems, you will pay nothing, or a small fee.

Neal: Do you think systems developers will offer their systems on the Internet for a monthly fee or for free instead of a lump sum payment?

Committee: I believe many system developers would like to receive a monthly income for their efforts. If thousands use a system, then this results in a profitable monthly income. If the small investor is faced with committing a large amount of his money for buying a system versus paying a monthly fee, he will choose the monthly fee. Because the Internet is causing a paradigm shift, this will force a change in the distribution channel.

Neal: Right now, there are a lot of people afraid of letting the computer do the trading for them. They don't want to lose everything if the computer malfunctions.

Committee: Presently, there are safeguards in on-line trading. For example, your account is always checked for sufficient funds before a trade is placed. I look at my entire portfolio at the end of the day, and then I decide how much money I allocate to each commodity for tomorrow's trading. Second, if I want to use stops to protect my gains, then I want the program to execute the stop at the price I set and not at the day's close or tomorrow's open. Third, I want a program that allows me to develop highly sophisticated system variables. Delphi allows me to do this.

Neal: What happens if you can't program?

Committee: You can always hire a programmer. In some parts of the country there are user groups for software. These groups meet every month and share ideas on programming and investing. There is a new concept brought forward by Digital Enterprises Ltd. Their software allows the investor to highlight data patterns, and then the program writes the system. Even if you have no programming skills, their program will write the appropriate system. That's amazing! The last option available to the nonprogrammer is to shop around and hire a CTA (commodity trader advisor). There are several thousand CTAs using various systems. By hiring a CTA, you gain not only a system but also a professional trader.

And currently, there are programs where you do not need to be a programmer. You first identify the computer, write the program, and then you just identify the trading pattern.

Neal: Yes, I have heard of those folks; they are located in New York. Do you have an easy system that you can share with us, any kind of pencil and paper system?

Committee: If the Chicago Cubs win, then go long corn the next day. If they lose, then go short. If they win both games of a doubleheader, then go long on corn and soybeans. If they lose both games, then go short on both. Close the positions at the end of the day.

Neal: That system would produce great results, and you know someone could sell it and call it a seasonal. . . . Okay, seriously, give us a quick-start version for evaluating a system.

Committee: First, if you can't get the maximum total drawdown and Sharpe Ratio on the system, then forget it. Second, use a system that works on a diversified portfolio of markets. I remember, when I got together with other system developers, how we all laughed at the single market systems that have 95% winning trades and made millions of dollars. We laugh because we know how to optimize a system that gives great historical results but is worthless in real-time trading. If it is a good system, it can trade many markets. Third, never buy a system that is a black box. A black box gives you trades but no rationale behind the trades. The investor should learn what works and what does not. If he knows the system, he can then either improve it or integrate it into other systems he's developing.

Notes from Neal: In trading Chicago style, every trader must have a system. It can be elaborate, computer-driven, or something as simple as getting the edge on customer orders. The discussion on risk should not deter people. If you are sincerely interested in how risk can torpedo your trading plan, I suggest the book *Against the Gods* by Peter Bernstein. I assign this book to many of the classes I teach.

Finally, keep in mind that if a system seems too good to be true, it most likely is.

MEAT IS CHEAP

Using the Internet is key when looking for trading ideas. Here is an Internet exchange I had with another trader. When trading the Chicago markets via computer, try to be part of a newsgroup. If you cannot locate one, you can try Markbrown.com or Omega-list@eskimo.com. This list tends to be Omega-oriented, but you can at least ask where the other newsgroups are that have your trading interests. These same newsgroups are vitally useful when purchasing software. Why not ask the Omega list what they think of TradeStation before you make a purchase?

It's a terrific way of getting a wide variety of opinions and just maybe the real truth.

Neal: What do you think of buying feeders down at these levels?

Kevin: It's kind of my thoughts compiled from tidbits of info I hear and read.

Neal: Okay, just give me your thoughts, but specifically on the feeders.

Kevin: I hate to trade feeders because of all the variables. My observations are from a couple of sources. My father is kind of semiretired and gets a kick out of driving a truck for a cattle buyer/feedlot operator. They normally spend a month in the fall hauling feeders out of Montana (six trucks, full-blast) to Nebraska and Kansas. This year they only made a couple of trips. The reason was that the ranchers would not take the price the feedlot guys would pay.

Couple of weeks later, I get a call (it was a referral) from a major corporation that also happens to run 5000 head of mother cows in Wyoming. For the first time in 100 years, they were planning on feeding out their calf production this year, due to low feeder prices.

Neal: That's great information.

Kevin: You put two and two together and surmise that feeders would actually be cheaper than they are had more feeders hit the market. I'm not sure how significant this is. Retained ownership in the feedlots has been picking up steam the last few years, and this is probably more piling on.

Neal: What about hogs?

Kevin: I read the article regarding the contract hogs on Bridge News last week. It makes sense. They are taking the vertically integrated model from poultry and using it on hogs. You've got these huge, closely held operations now, like Premium Standard (owned by Continental), National Farms (Bass Brothers), and Seaboard. The first two are just producers, but Seaboard is completely vertical, with contract growers. Seaboard runs a big poultry operation in the Southeast and is doing the same thing with hogs in Oklahoma, Kansas, and Colorado. They will *never* disclose what they are actually paying for hogs from their company-owned and contract grower sources.

Neal: You sound bearish.

Kevin: I predict a new round of bankrupt producers and the resulting credit crunch in the AG sector, which will push prices lower yet. I hope I'm wrong.

The short answer is: Probably lower than you think. You asked about feeders and hogs.

Feeder cattle is always a subjective market and is influenced by factors that you would not normally think of. Feeders are part of the basic formula FC + Corn = LC. Also, if there is abundant pasture, there will be a big demand for feeders, to put them on grass awhile. Conversely, if there is a drought, they will all get dumped on the market. That's an example. There are a hundred other things. My impression is that this year, many ranchers are unwilling to take the price bid for feeders, so they are retaining ownership right into the feedlot. To take it a step further, had they sold the feeders, the prices would be lower than they are now.

Now, regarding lean hogs: this morning they are quoting live hog prices in Iowa at 8.50 to 13.50 $/cwt (that's $21.25 to $33.75 for a 250-lb hog). If you assume a 74% dress, that's a lean hog price of 11.50 to 18.25. February futures are trading 30.07. If cash does not rally, I would expect the futures to drop. The big premiums in the back month LH futures are really bearish for the hog complex in general; it sends all the wrong signals to the market.

As I understand the problem in general, many of the large hog producers (factory farms) have a contract with the packers for X amount of hogs at a fixed price (with some adjustments). I read last week that the contract price is in the high $30.00s/cwt on a live basis (divide by 0.74 for LH price). With the current price of wholesale pork cuts, the packers basically have let the price drop (on noncontract hogs) to get to a break-even on kill margins. According to the article I read last week, if a packer is killing 40% contract hogs, they are close to break-even overall by paying current prices for the remaining 60% of the kill.

I buy a lot of bottled water (I spend time in the boonies), and the cheapest I've found is at Wal-Mart for 50 cents a gallon. That would be $24.00 per barrel (to compare with crude oil), and crude is trading for $11.00—and that's for the good crude.

I'm buying gas for 74 cents a gallon, and that includes 38 cents of road tax. So I could buy tax-exempt gas for 36 cents a gallon. Too bad we can't drink gas. My wife made chicken noodle soup the other night, with a whole chicken. After I complimented her on the fine meal, she mentioned that the bread for the meal cost more than the meat.

China announced that they will produce 501 to 503 million metric tons (MMTs) of grain this year, which is just shy of the record 504 MMTs produced in 1996. And this is with record flooding.

Remember last summer when the President announced all the grain giveaways? Well, of the little tonnage that has shipped, it was reexported for cash.

It really makes you wonder what it will take to break the cycle. With all the cash being pumped into financial assets, it makes you wonder how they will perform should commodity prices ever start to rise.

Neal: Commodities may be starting the next bull market.

DOUG PATRICK

You Could Live off My Mistakes

Doug has spent over 10,000 hours programming and checking out every conceivable trading system. Though his concept of trading Chicago-style relies on sending real-time signals to subscribers, his overview of the Chicago markets is focused and accurate. Doug and I first met after he purchased Pivot Point software from me. Later we learned that we both work with the same software programmer.

Residing in Boca Raton, Florida, Doug does not have to brave the Chicago elements, but to trade the Chicago markets, he definitely decided to be a system trader.

Neal: Doug, you seem to be a big believer in not following the crowd when trading.

Doug: Follow the crowd and always be confused; that is what I say. Every day, we hear about market sentiment and how it pertains to the future course of prices. To many bulls it's bearish, and to many bears it's bullish. The problem arises in determining how many is too many and whether they are long-term bullish or short-term bullish, looking for a correction or some trend change. The problem compounds when we try to actually trade on the information. A little-known fact is that 75% of analysts were bearish at the top of the 1929 market. The problem was that most were short-term bearish. This is why most of the public tends to buy the dips as a market declines in a bear market. Each wave of selling is viewed as another buying opportunity, and by the time the realization that something more than a correction is going on, it's too late.

Neal: But isn't the secret to making money managing information?

Doug: I talk to traders every day and am always amazed at the difference in results using the same information. I have traders using the system who have made money during the recent poor trading market and others who lost money during trades that yielded doubles and triples. I have traders who have suggested that I use them as a contrary indicator. I've always contended that if we use good money management and consistent adherence to a quality system, the results should be the same for everyone. The reality couldn't be further from the truth. I firmly believe that we get what we focus on the most. The problem is that most of us spend our time focusing on what we don't want. Let's say we don't want to lose money. By focusing on ways of not losing money, in reality, we get just that. The subconscious tends to be very literal and will give you exactly what it thinks you want. In this case, by focusing on losing money your subconscious believes that's what you want and causes you to lose money. Another good example is the system we use. What if we choose to focus on the 30% losing trades and ignore the 70% winning trades. Do you think anyone would be successful? Of course not. We must always focus on winning the war, and not the battle.

Neal: Well, you sound like a market guru.

Doug: In October of 1987, I was certain that the market was in for a 500- to 600-point down day. I was so certain that I had told everyone I knew, and my entire family. I was so certain that when I placed my order on the Thursday before the 1987 crash, I cut the order in half and only bought 25 contracts instead of the 50 I intended to buy. My fear cost me $125,000. Even though I believed with every fiber of my being that I was right, my fear of being wrong caused me to become cautious at the worst possible time. Was I being objective? Of course not. Being objective allows you to see the market as it is. You must put emotion, fear, and greed in the background to have any chance of consistently beating the market. We are constantly bombarded with information that contradicts our research, opinions, observations, and decisions. We must enter each trade with blinders on. With the objectivity to come to an informed decision and the discipline to carry out that decision, you will be on your way to consistent trading profits. So you see, I am not that much of a guru.

Neal: Someone once said trading is a difficult way to make an easy buck.

Doug: Trading isn't easy, and creating an objective, disciplined mindset to trade from is paramount in developing winning trading habits. If you're having trouble being successful at trading or you seem to always be fearful and full of doubt, the first place to look is at yourself. Our tendency is to take a mechanical process that we may have spent months or even years perfecting and try to make decisions based on emotions that may be counter to our plan or system. Even if you're right on occasion, not following your trading plan will result in frustration and losses over time.

Neal: If it looks like a duck, walks like a duck, and quacks like a duck, it must be a chicken. Is that what you're saying?

Doug: How many times have you been told that a piece of news is bullish, only to find a few weeks later that the same news is now bearish. Welcome to the world of smoke and mirrors. As humans, we believe that there must be a reason that the market moves. In reality, there are millions of reasons at any given moment why a market moves. The market is in constant motion, as is the information that drives our opinions. Always remember that for every buyer, there is a seller, and both have determined at that moment that their action is the correct action. In the long run, you'll find that news has very little lasting effect on the market, and ultimately the market will move in the direction of least resistance. The best lesson we can learn is to spend our time listening to the market rather than rationalizing the market.

Neal: Trading the Chicago markets means a system to you?

Doug: A trading system or method, in effect, creates an objective, consistent frame from which to make your trading decisions. Emotion and lack of discipline are the primary reasons that most traders fail. The market doesn't know us personally, nor is there a conspiracy by some secret organization to take our money away. In reality, we as humans are our own worst enemy when it comes to making informed decisions. Our emotions tend to dictate our judgment. A system will bring our actions into sync with the reality of the moment. A good system obviously will.

Neal: Look, why not use stop-loss orders and forget the system?

Doug: Stop-loss orders are designed to keep a small losing trade from becoming a large losing trade. This falls under "preservation of capital" and money management. First, what is a stop-loss order? A stop-loss can take many forms, but some of the more common ones are money management, trailing, break-even, and % trailing. A money management stop is nothing more than determining a price below your entry price where you would sell your position if reached. With a trailing stop, your goal is to lock in a profit by taking yourself out of a trade if the index drops a specified amount from a print high or low. A break-even stop is exactly what it sounds like. If your trade drops to your entry price, it takes you out of the trade. A break-even stop should be used in conjunction with other stops because if you haven't moved above your entry price, the stop will never be triggered. A trailing % stop is the same as a trailing stop, but it uses a % instead of a specific point amount. All of these types of stops have advantages and disadvantages. You must carefully weigh the system or method you use for trading to determine the type or types of stops that will work.

Neal: I know, Doug, that you also trade options. Why?

Doug: Leverage is why we trade options in the first place. For those of you who have been following us for a while, you know that we tend to recommend the current month expiration options that cluster around $5. Why do we do this?

Over the years, we've learned that our best trades come from the options that have the highest volume. Volume serves several functions. Number 1, it provides us liquidity or a market for our options. Number 2, it provides us with the leverage to overcome the natural tendency of options to lose value over time, or time premium. Number 3, it gives us a fair playing field. The more active an option is, the smaller the spread between the bid and ask, and thus the less likely we are to get a bad fill. Many novice traders are under the misconception that buying options out two or three months will give them safety. In reality, the only way to overcome the deterioration of time premium is to shorten your holding period. As you get closer to expiration, your leverage increases dramatically, as does your risk. As long as you are managing your trades properly, with good money management, your risk/reward far outweighs the inherent risk of trading an option that is expiring soon.

Neal: You cannot use a system to trade options, or can you?

Doug: Options and other short-term trading vehicles' current prices are determined by demand or lack of demand, and demand is determined by expectation of the future. When the market is making little progress up or down, traders are unwilling to bid prices up because their expectations are low. The prices on both puts and calls will slowly adjust lower, creating options that are below fair value. Once a move begins, the options that reflect the direction of the move will rapidly move to an overpriced condition, and the options that are in the other direction will move further into undervalued range. If you try to buy when the market is in a fast trading condition, the demand is high to own and low to sell and you'll pay a premium to own the option. Let's say that you bought a put on the close and the market is moving sharply to the downside. You are buying in anticipation of even lower prices. The seller is feeling the same emotion and is only willing to sell if you pay a premium that reflects his expectation. If, the next morning, the market opens down, but not to the degree that the trader expected, the puts will actually lose value and the calls may increase. We at Crash Proof Advisors are aware of this phenomenon and time not only the market but also the trade.

Neal: You know so many folks. Tell me about their huge gains; tell me about one of your losing days.

Doug: The year was 1982 and I had caught a fantastic down move. I was sitting on a $45,000 profit and looking for more. The market started to turn up, but being the gifted technician that I thought I was, I felt that this was a minor blip and that the bear market would continue. Day after day, the market continued to rise, and my profits began to erode. Logic told me that the market had to turn down soon. The market continued to rise for 17 days in a row. The period that followed was the greatest bull market in history.

Neal: So you turned a $45,000 winner into a $5000 loser.

Doug: Exactly.

Neal: No wonder you are a system trader.

Doug: Yes.

Neal: Where do you see on-line trading going in the future?

Doug: I see the growth in on-line trading continuing into the 21st century. As more and more people discover the Internet, they will also discover the convenience of placing orders on-line. With this growth, the need for high-quality trading information will also grow. We are working hard to create products and tools for the future. We have been learning along with other Internet-based companies that speed of signal delivery and rapid order fills are top priorities for any successful trader. We are currently experimenting with real-time trading rooms complete with automated instant signal delivery and chat between traders.

My vision of the future shows a trader sitting in front of his computer, with a real-time trading room tailored to his market style and market type. Traders will be able to interact with other traders with similar interests. Signals will be posted as soon as they are generated to their computers, and an order will be able to be placed without ever leaving the trading room. These rooms will be available 24 hours a day, making 24-hour trading a reality. We are very close to making this vision a reality now.

Neal: In closing, is there any advice you'd like to give other traders who may want to follow in your footsteps and develop their own trading systems?

Doug: First and foremost, observe, observe, observe. All winning trading systems are based on a sound concept. Too many system designers begin by looking for the magic indicator that's going to make them rich. It doesn't exist. Instead, observe the market, get to know your chosen market, and look for repeating patterns or combinations of factors that seem to have predictive value. Then try to explain why these patterns or factors may work. I'm not a big believer in doing computer searches and statistical fits. The markets are much too dynamic for these searches to reveal more than a data fit over a specified time period. These types of systems will usually fall apart as soon as you try to use them on real trading. Unfortunately, the financial papers are littered with these systems, claiming riches beyond your wildest dreams. If a system doesn't produce good results over many time periods and market types, avoid it like the plague. Let's say you've got the concept and it makes sense; now what? Now you work. As an example, the systems I use took four years to develop and test, and they are still a work in progress. It takes, in many cases, thousands of hours to program, test, change, retest, and so on, before you may have a system that makes money in real-time trading. I know that there are those who would lead you to believe that this is not the case, but this has been my experience. If you are unwilling to give system development this kind of dedication and time, leave it to others. If, however, you have what it takes, you will find it to be one of the most satisfying things you'll ever do.

Neal: Wow! That was a mouthful. How can traders reach you?

Doug: Here is my name and business address:

Doug Patrick
Crash Proof Advisors, Inc.
5820 North Federal Hwy., Suite D4
Boca Raton, Florida 33487

Phone: (561) 988-2364
Fax: (561) 994-4640

Home: (561) 368-8875
URL: www.crashproofadvisors.com
E-mail: webmaster@crashproofadvisors.com
Or: pdp@gate.net

Pit Stops

Now Behave Yourself

The chaos you see in the trading pit is regulated. You can get a ticket. These are rules taken from the CBOT rule book.

Any member or individual with floor access privileges who has received a Pit Committee ticket for decorum offense of disorderly conduct, intentional physical abuse, sexual harassment, and/or use of profane or obscene language and during the same session, engages in a further rule or regulation violation relating to disorderly conduct, intentional physical abuse, sexual harassment, and/or use of profane or obscene language may, in addition to other sanctions (including but not limited to fines, suspensions, and expulsions imposed by the Association, pursuant to the rules and regulations), be immediately and summarily removed from the exchange trading floor and denied trading floor access for the remainder of the trading session, pursuant to the following procedures:

a. Certification by a chairman of the Pit Committee (or in the chairman's absence, by a vice-chairman of the Pit Committee) that the individual has continued to engage in disorderly conduct, intentional physical abuse, sexual harassment, and/or use of profane or obscene language after having previously received a Pit Committee ticket for the same offense in the same trading session.

b. Approval of such summary action by a member of the Floor Governors Committee and a member of the Board of Directors or by two members of the Board of Directors, provided that no individual granting such approval shall have been in the altercation.

Additionally, should the first such offense be of such a serious nature, the individual may be denied trading floor access for the duration of the trading session pursuant to that above procedure. (03/01/97)

Comment: There is an order in the chaos you see in the pits. Actually, trading Chicago style is more than hot, sweaty men in the pit. It is based on "keeping your word" and integrity when making trades.

Pit Stops

SuperCharts

As we all know, the S&P futures tend to retrace, then shoot ahead; retrace, then shoot ahead. Here is an approach that takes advantage of this action by buying only after the market has fallen and started to move up again. It will catch some of the big moves and do better than break even on the rest.

This system *buys* when the S&P corrects 4% and then goes up. It *sells* if (a) it rises 4%, (b) it drops 4%, or (c) it crosses below a parabolic. You may want to try this on the Dow Jones Industrial Average futures. In Chicago-style trading, buying dips and selling rallies is part of the way we trade. Just be sure that you exit when the market goes against you. The SuperChart code is as follows:

IF: C[1] < .96 * HIGHEST(H,15)[1] and c > c[1] then: BUY this bar on the Close

IF: C < .96 * (EntryPrice) OR C CROSSES BELOW PARABOLIC(.00175)

OR maxPositionProfit > .04 * EntryPrice then: EXITLONG next bar at the market.

I was told that this approach had 78% accuracy. But keep in mind that we have just experienced a great bull market. As in any system, know what has been going on in the market you are testing.

What if you are not a programmer? Well, good news. There is software readily available in which the computer will write the code. All you have to do is identify key patterns. Currently, a company in New York allows traders to merely describe and locate a pattern. No written code required.

The application allows a trader to visually paint a market situation and then create an indicator or trading system by clicking a button. Since many traders are visually oriented, this is superior to most software packages with which you must learn programming skills just to trade.

Contact: webmaster@digital-ltd.com

CHUCK THOMPSON

WE ALL LOVE THE DATA VENDOR

C huck Thompson is chief technology officer and senior vice-president of marketing for DBC. Mr. Thompson's views are significant in light of the future of trading Chicago style and receiving data from various vendors.

Neal: It has been said that trading is managing information. How can traders possibly manage all the information that is available during the trading day?

Chuck: Unless they have a good data vendor and software, they can't. There are over 8 million trades and quotes per day to manage. DBC servers collect all that for the user. The user is not loading a CD with gigabytes of data on his PC; he uses DBC history servers with over 10 GB of daily data.

Neal: What are the advantages of receiving data from DBC rather than CQG or Future Source?

Chuck: DBC's latest technology is two-way; they are one-way broadcast. A user can, upon demand, download a 10-year chart, every tick on a stock since it opened, as soon as he starts his system from anywhere in the world on the Internet. It's not limited, like those other systems, to a single location. Plus the prices are lower, less than 50% of the cost—and faster.

Neal: You must have various software vendors trying to have you promote their software. How do you stay impartial?

Chuck: Easy, we promote the most popular package with our users. We are interested in the ones that our users find work for them.

Neal: Is the Internet a threat to your business? For example, I can get quotes from the net for only $20.00 per month.

Chuck: No, the Internet is the best thing that ever happened to DBC. We have the fastest, most economical system for streaming real-time quotes.

LARRY EHRHART

Why Software That Works May Not Be the One

When Market Profile was developed here in Chicago, Larry Ehrhart was one of the first researchers and traders to see its potential. He has been a guest speaker at the Chicago Mercantile Exchange. Larry and I have known each other for nearly 11 years. He takes his work very seriously and works with his clients on a one-on-one basis. He is sort of a one-man band, and it is great to speak with someone who trades with the software he developed.

Neal: Your software is so logical and so natural to the Chicago style of trading, I wonder why you are not more popular?

Larry: I think part of the reason is that I am a trader who wrote software for my own trading, whereas the competition set out with programmers to develop software to sell. I do very little advertising. Second, Market Profile (which I emphasize) does not provide what most newbies want. They want an indicator that tells them what to do. I believe that neither you nor I could develop a mechanical system that would work long-term; if so, we'd own the world in a short time. So my approach is to stress psychology of trading, money management, and using various tools to improve what is basically a throw of the dart. This "gut feel" trading approach is not for everyone.

Neal: Maybe you should make wild claims or something.

Larry: No comment!

Neal: Seriously, will your software help day-traders?

Larry: Definitely. And even swing traders are day-traders when they get in and out. WINdoTRADEr provides a lot of information on the character of the markets. It uses color and/or numbers to show where the tick volume is. It's almost like hearing the yelling on the floor.

Neal: Can you give a specific example and how you would identify a good trade?

Larry: Figure 21-1 can't be fully explained in a sentence, but it shows March 99 TBonds for parts of December 29 and 30. The boxes and numbers in the upper left are for December 30, and the columns of numbers in the middle and right are a five-minute bar chart for part of December 29. The bar from 127-10 to 127-14 under the fourth letter at the top (*I*) is a high-volume squat (it had 37 ticks and was also a key reversal bar). Five bars later (the third *J*) was also a high-volume squat (41 ticks and a key reversal).

These bars were highs of the day when they formed. They showed the market running into resistance, with a lot of volume. They *should have* caused the market to reverse. The fact that the market fought through this heavy resistance was a clear indication that the market would move to higher levels. As a day-trader, I would have stopped fading the market when the first squat failed and would have had a long bias the next day. If I were a swing trader who decided to go long December 29, for

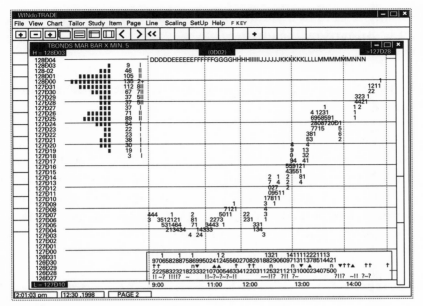

FIGURE 21-1. WTTieBar.GIF.

whatever reason, I should have had more confidence based on this failure of the squats and perhaps put on a larger position than normal. The swing trader would also have found the price levels where the big guys play and might well have considered stops based on this activity rather than a money stop.

Neal: The terms you use, like *squat*, would you be kind enough to explain them?

Larry: A *squat* (shown as a double exclamation point) is an increase in volume and a decrease in the MFI from one bar to the next. The MFI is the range of a bar divided by its volume. If the volume increases more than the range, then the MFI goes down, suggesting resistance (or support). There is more activity, but the market is moving less proportionately. If the volume increases significantly and is high in and of itself for that commodity, it suggests the big players are now involved. That tug-of-war usually results in a sudden move (generally a reversal); the market is "squatting," ready to leap.

Neal: What type of futures trader would obtain your software?

Larry: Someone who wants Market Profile charting or someone who trades by gut feel. If you watch only a handful of markets intently all day, you become quite used to things like how frequently each trades, how much range typically occurs in, say, five minutes, and so forth. WINdoTRADEr lets you see this information more readily than typical OHLC charts.

Neal: Larry, I am sure people would want to learn more. Please give us your e-mail address.

Larry: Wintrade@windotrader.com.

Pit Stops

From the Pits to the PC

Tom Rehberger and I traded with each other at the Mid-America Commodity Exchange. He was in an arbitrage group that kept the Chicago Board of Trade and Mid Am-Bond pit in check. After two in the afternoon, the Mid-Am had paper coming from locals and cash dealers. Tom told me about the 1000-lot trade he did. Well, so much for people who say there is no liquidity at the Mid-America. Tom has made the transition from the pit to the PC. He also incorporates many of the skills learned from his pit trading days. I asked Tom to share his best system, but he had a better idea. This pit stop is a must-read.

Tom: I was asked to share my best system idea that people could use immediately in their trading. I replied that I would do one better and share what I think are the most important dynamics common to all the successful trading systems and floor traders that I have encountered in my career. I'm thoroughly enjoying the success that the systems had this last year and am looking forward to what this year will bring. I hope you will find this information useful as we trade our way through the new year.

I have followed one rule in my search for trading strategies in this extremely difficult business: Find the people who are making money and learn how they earn that money. In a business where an estimated 90% of the people lose money, it's not an easy quest. To make matters worse, charlatans abound.

At the core of all successful trading systems are two dynamics, momentum and statistics. The first dynamic is simple to understand and use. You can't make money unless the markets are moving. If it's not trending, you're guessing, and futures don't pay dividends so there is no reward for taking a position and waiting. Most profitable systems will be in on the same trend, some earlier, some later, but they all need the price momentum to be profitable. The second dynamic, statistics, is hard love. Trading systems consist of many trades. It is not necessary for each trade to be profitable. To be profitable, your system needs to be right more, or to larger degree, than it is wrong. I learned this after a couple of months of standing in the pits with no clue of how to make money. A big trader tapped me on the shoulder and said, "Hey kid, make a hundred trades and then come talk to me!" I thought he was crazy or trying to get rid of me. But I took that little piece of advice and it kept me trading on the floor for eight years. You can't judge anything from one trade; after 100, you have a plan. And after a thousand trades, there is nothing you have not seen. Trading involves drawdowns and runups in equity, and you have to deal with them both to trade. Don't get stuck in the trap of trying to eliminate all of the drawdowns, which would be just as unrealistic as extrapolating only the winning trades into a projected return.

Tom's #1 Rule for Trading: If you buy the highs and sell the lows, you will collect all of the winners and miss some of the losers. This simple rule swings the probabilities in your favor and helps to limit the big negative outliers. If you place an order under the market to buy, you will own all of the losers and miss some of the winners (same for sells above the market). This swings the probabilities against you and makes your job harder.

The money in trading is made by taking away the opportunity from somebody else. It's a very competitive sport. If you were trading on the floor and it was 4 bid at 5 and 5s are trading, would you buy them or sell them? Buy them! Be the first 5 bid! Now it's 5 bid at 6 and you can offer 6s. You would have participated in one of many "mini" trends that make up the daily trading on the floor. Trading systems look for breakouts of some sort to signal the beginning or existence of a trend. Whether it goes from 4 to 6 or 400 to 600, the principle is the same.

Although this concept of going with the trend is common to many markets as well as futures trading, some people adapt to it more easily than others do. I think it's one of the reasons some people have so much trouble trading. I hope this idea can help you adjust to the frame of mind that you need to trade. If you are looking for systems that use these ideas, you can contact me at PMB Inc., (800) 598-0631, or at systems@pmbinc.com.

Neal: Choosing the right pit, getting trades, taking profits and losses, and adding to a profit are not only pit skills, they are trading skills.

When you step in the pit, you try to look at the outside market action and get a handle on what the locals are doing. You also want to know if the big doggies are hot or if they are cold. In this case the big doggies are the big traders. If you can translate these concepts into a portion of your system trading, you will be well on your way to trading Chicago style off the floor.

Also, did you notice how similar Tom Rehberger's comments are to CV's? (See Chapter 9.)

MARK KELSEY

Back to the Futures Pit, but Without the Lobster

Mark Kelsey and I first met when he was a trader at the Mid-America Commodity Exchange. Mark not only works with customers but also trades for himself. He has both pit and broker experience.

Neal: How did you get started in the business?

Mark: I started out at the Kansas City Board of Trade. The Value Line was just taking off, and I was a phone clerk on the trading floor. After the crash of 1987, the Value Line dried up and it was time for me to move on. I decided that I had to be where the pot was boiling, so I left Kansas City and headed to the source of commodities, Chicago.

Neal: So what did you do?

Mark: I started pounding the pavement, and eventually I was offered a job with Pru-Bach as an assistant in their options trading group. I hated it. To me, futures were fast and exciting, but options were slow and methodical. Naturally, it wasn't until years later that I realized just how much I had learned about options during my short stay. And though I learned a great deal about options early, for my first ten years I rarely ever used the knowledge. Only staying with Pru-Bach for about nine months, I confidently decided it was time to trade for myself. I bought a Mid-Am seat for $9000, and the next three years was an enormous learning experience for me.

Neal: Do you prefer trading on the floor or off the floor?

Mark: Well, it's really apples and oranges. First of all, the pit is a difficult place to understand. The way I think of it is exciting, no-holds-barred, in-your-face, Chicago-style trading. When you are trading in the pit, you stand next to the same guys and trade with the same people day in and day out. You find yourself in a very rich pool of information. The pit is a crowded arena of yelling, screaming, gesturing, and shoving, all for what are basically a few ticks of action. For the most part, 50% of the time you are standing around just waiting for something to happen, and when it does, you had better be ready for the ride. It's an emotionally and physically draining experience, especially for the younger traders.

On the other hand, off-the-floor trading is a much calmer experience, externally. There are no other traders jockeying for a position, no other traders wanting to sell to the same trader you are trying to sell to. Most of the day is made up looking over charts and determining trading opportunities. And you go home a lot less bruised.

Neal: Okay, Mark, ten grinding years on the floor and what did you really learn about trading Chicago style?

Mark: Simple. Every trader was a failure early. There is a story about Charlie D., who made tens of millions of dollars trading. In his first few months, he lost half of his trading equity in a single day. For the next two months, he sat on the sidelines watching the interrelationships of the markets, and obviously he learned something. Every trader I have ever worked with has had the same type of experience. My mentor, an S&P trader, lost $180,000 during his first three years, before he even made a penny. He then went on the make, over $1 million per year since 1991. My point is this: Your first few years are a learning experience; no more, no less. Regardless of whether you make $10,000 or lose $10,000 during your first few years, if you can survive the experience, you will be a better trader because of it.

So, working with so many traders, I started noticing a pattern of success and failure. As it turns out, successful investors have at least five things in common. And traders who experience failure have at least five things in common.

Neal: What are all of these things in common?

Mark: Let's start with the successful traders and talk about their commonalities. Successful traders *generally trade a specific market or a group of markets that are related.* An example is the S&Ps and the bonds or, as a group, the financials. They tend to *get out of bed every morning and already know how they're going to trade for the day.*

1. They have an absolute trading strategy and follow it to the letter.
2. They find something that works for them and do it over and over, like a cookie-cutting concept.
3. They are emotionally, physically, and financially capitalized; consequently, they are not afraid of risking small amounts of money. They have more information. They tend to have access to quotes and upcoming reports.
4. They don't talk about trading; they just do it.
5. They focus on the trading aspect, not the money, because the money will take care of itself.

As a rule, they are much better outfitted for success!

Now we come to the unsuccessful traders. I have found that their factor of failure is that they make and repeat the same mistakes over and over . . . because they never learn from them.

1. It's usually a discipline problem that encompasses small profits and big losses.
2. They tend to have little or no trading strategy.
3. They are undercapitalized.
4. They generally spend as little as possible on gathering market information.
5. They blame others for their losses.

Neal: Now that you are on the retail side of the business, how do you feel you can help your customers?

Mark: I believe that my job as a trading broker is to move them up the trading ladder, to show them what they're missing in terms of their trading skills, and to enhance their overall trading ability. I also try to outfit my customers. With almost fifteen years of experience, I have made every mistake in the book. I can relate to everything my customers are thinking and feeling because I was once in their shoes. I can tell a lot about someone in the first fifteen minutes of conversation. Different investors have different maturity levels, and very few are actually complete traders.

Neal: Tell me more about the different levels of trading maturity.

Mark: When new traders first start out, they want to try to buy low and sell high, thinking that picking tops and bottoms is the correct way to trade. There's no faster way to the poorhouse. The joke on the floor is, "Top pickers and bottom pickers become cotton pickers."

In this first level of trading, the investor can only see small profits. What I try to help them learn is to let their profits ride and to cut their losses early. In this stage, they almost always trade only futures, and only on very short moves.

Second-level investors usually have two or three years of trading experience, have already made some of the most crucial mistakes, and have learned from them. These are some of the best traders because they are well-disciplined. These are my favorite kinds of traders; they have the basic understanding of how the market works and are eager to learn the more-complicated nuances of trading.

The third-level trader has exhausted the basic learning experience of futures trading and is ready to dabble in options. Most have also had some experience in stock trading. One point I make to them is how different stock options and futures options are. With stock options, the momentum is usually to the upside, and the trend will carry the market. With commodities, the options are designed to decay. They are simply used as an insurance policy for a range-bound market. Therefore, 90% of all options go off the board worthless. Consequently, traders must use an option strategy which requires the buying and selling of puts and calls simultaneously. Most investors have a difficult time understanding this concept until they reach the third level of trading experience.

The final level, the fourth level, is what I call the "complete trader." These traders are much more sophisticated and use futures and options together for what are known as "synthetic trades."

Neal: You mentioned "outfitting" your customers. What did you mean?

Mark: Technology has come a long way. Today, you can actually be an off-the-floor pit trader. Technology allows you to be as close to the pit as possible without actually being in it. You no longer need a seat to have the edge. For example, you can be on a beach in Hawaii and have close to the same advantage as the trader who is standing directly in the pit—if you know what to look for.

I outfit my customers by showing them how the real professionals trade. For example, five years ago, real-time quotes via a computer system like CQG cost an arm and a leg. Now you can pick them up for a couple hundred dollars a month. And a "squawk box," which gives live audio quotes from the pit, was unheard of for the masses. The larger institutional and commercial traders were the only ones who could afford it, for it cost a few thousand dollars a month back then. Today, that same squawk box can be in every home for about $100 a month. It's an advantage every serious off-the-floor trader needs, yet few people know it's available or where to get it. And finally, on-line trading has come of age. Trades can be sent directly to the pit from your home computer, to a handheld modular unit, and trades can be filled in as little as three seconds.

Neal: Do you have any trading strategies that you use?

Mark: Absolutely. I'll show you a way to pinpoint your trading so you can use precision accuracy to make a trade. It works on all markets, even stocks. First of all, remember that the markets only have three directions: up, down, and sideways. Your job is to decide what trend the market is in at any given time. For example, the market will repeat the same signals over and over if it is an uptrend.

Here's a trading strategy for S&Ps. First, take a look at the last 10 trading ranges. Take all of those ranges and add them together; you should get something like 13,000 or 14,000. Then take that same number and divide by 10, you should get 1300 or 1400. However, to keep it simple, we will use 1000. Assuming that the daily range for the S&P is 1000, we already have a good idea where the support and resistance is and where we will make our first trade of the day. Let's also assume that the S&Ps are in an uptrend, as they are about 70% of the time. Using simple Fibonacci retracement, 33%, 50%, and 66%, which is the cornerstone of Fibonacci, we then would assume that our first trade would be to buy at the 33% retracement. We would also put our sell stop just below the 50% retracement. In a true uptrending market, the price rarely goes below the 50% retracement. Furthermore, if that same market went below 66% retracement, it could be a good signal of a countermove to the downside. If all goes well, I will want to take profit at the upper 50% retracement. We could repeat this same trade over and over. Let the markets come to you; don't chase them. If the S&Ps are at 1010.00, our first buy signal will be around 1006.60, and we would put the sale stop at 1004.80. We then want to take profit at 1015.00. If the market traded below 1003.30, it could be a good indication of a change in the trend.

Just a little note: Keep your eye on the open interest. In a long-term rally, the open interest should increase with the rise of the markets. If the trading range increases and the open interest doesn't, keep your eyes open for a larger countermove to the downside.

Neal: Any final thoughts?

Mark: I would just say to keep your focus wide and take a look at the big picture. One trading day doesn't make a career. Don't try to go for the big kill, or you could wind up on the wrong side of the trade.

Mark can be reached at (773) 588-6636.

RUSSELL WASENDORF

24-Hour Markets Are Not Really New

Russell R. Wasendorf, Sr. is chairman and chief executive officer of PFG, Inc., a futures commission merchant. He also heads Wasendorf & Associates, Inc., a research firm specializing in managed futures investment, and is president of Wasendorf & Son Company.

Since 1980, he has written and published the highly acclaimed market letter *Futures and Options Factors*. He was the past director of the Commodity Education Institute and founder of the Center for Futures Education.

I asked Russell to share his thoughts on the future of technology and trading.

Neal: It is becoming obvious that the average trader has as much access to information as the broker does. Why will traders need brokers to trade in the future? Or will they? Your thoughts please.

Russ: For over a century, the futures industry has endeavored to provide detailed "state of the art" information about futures markets. A keynote of the futures industry has been dissemination of salient supply and demand of the underlying commodities. Therefore, it is not totally unusual for traders to have access to a wide variety of information and statistics about individual markets.

For the recent decades, even a novice trader could, with very little effort, access information used by professional traders. Therefore, the abundance of information available to the general public through the Internet and other electronic means does not necessarily ring a death knell for the broker. The endless supply of information may actually enhance or increase the need for someone with the ability to filter and distill the information into a useful form. Certainly the clerk function of the broker will diminish, since the task of order entry and execution can be accomplished electronically.

It has been my experience that there is no substitute for experience when it comes to trading the markets profitably. The customer can either gain that experience through the expense of time, money, and considerable effort or associate himself or herself with a mentoring broker.

Neal: Technology is great for trading the Chicago markets, but how are traders going to adjust to a 24-hour market?

Russ: I have never thought of markets being anything other than 24-hour markets. In the past, we may have had the opportunity to express our opinion financially *only* within the confines of the narrow trading hours of a specific market. But even twenty-five years ago, when I was singularly concerned with the soybean market, our first concern each day was to review Rotterdam, Holland, prices. Even then, we were conscious of the price determination in other parts of the world affecting the price determination in the trading pits. Twenty-four-hour markets acknowledge that the sun never sets on the process of price determination in virtually every market.

During recent years, markets have become electronically available. Acknowledging this fact, Chicago markets have made their clearing capabilities available to an electronic version of the pit-traded markets. In actual practice, this is not an earth-shaking change. Traders have long been accustomed to trading markets for a specific segment of time. Individuals who day-trade markets are in and out within the same day. Certainly there is a version of this trading electronically in night sessions. Position traders have been accustomed to trading overnight surprises for decades. The only difference now is that they can actually do something about it by placing protective orders in the electronic sessions. Now position traders can more adequately protect their exchange-traded market positions. I believe it is actually a mistake for traders to think of the overnight markets as a threat to their procedures—to fear that there is someone "fooling around" with their markets while they are asleep. The truth is that there has always been market activity while some traders slumber, but this is not necessarily a concern that requires a vast adjustment.

Neal: Since markets are linked together, it won't be uncommon to watch big moves happen on weekends, while the Chicago markets are closed. This type of risk can play havoc with brokerage firms.

Russ: Big moves always play havoc with brokerage firms, whether they occur while some markets are open or closed. Certainly the futures commission merchant (FCM) has been forced to adjust to a variety of new risks during recent decades, and there are no simple answers. Electronic markets and other computerization of the futures industry actually provide for greater opportunities for more precise risk management.

As our firm created electronic order-entry capabilities, I adamantly insisted that risk management characteristics must be an integral part. Restrictions to prevent a customer from placing orders without adequate funds is a serious concern.

Yet there is simply no way an FCM can avoid unknown market risks. Computerization has at least allowed the FCM to react more quickly and in many cases to prevent risks of the unknown from decimating the firm.

Neal: There are different laws regulating futures in different countries. How is a firm going to "know the customer" or know when the client is trading off their trading profile?

Russ: Fortunately, as regulations develop worldwide, foreign regulators have been adopting many of the elements of the U.S. regulatory model. Even in those cases where regulation is not uniform between different international jurisdictions, we have discovered that the law of the jurisdiction where an order was executed will often prevail. Actually, the international laws designed to suppress drug trade have been useful in domesticating judgments in a foreign jurisdiction.

I anticipate that as activities on the Internet and other international commerce become more common, then international law will make appropriate adjustments. As an FCM, we recognize that regardless of the customer, there is no substitute for intensive risk management. Regardless of the origin of the customer, the FCM must recognize the age-old rule that every margin check is good except the last one. Therefore, the intensive adherence to risk management procedures will make up for the inability to know everything about the customer.

Neal: What criteria should traders use when choosing a computer on-line trading brokerage firm?

Russ: The process of choosing a computer on-line system is not vastly different than the process of selecting a broker. Certainly the most important element is the comfort level that the trader has with the system itself. Obviously, the system must be able to handle all of the types of orders that the trader is accustomed to using, and it should access all of the markets the trader trades. Beyond the personal comfort level, there are a number of features some on-line systems have that enhance the trader's ability to trade and protect the trader from potential "computer bugs," while providing speedy order entry and execution. Enhancements include features such as on-line equity runs, marked-to-the-market "tick by tick" position margin and equity information, and personal real-time management reports (such as lists of filled orders, resting orders, and open orders). It is important for some customers to easily cancel orders or to check the status of orders placed earlier.

Additional enhancements include real-time market quotes, market news, and charting capabilities. Even if the order-entry service does not provide these mechanisms, it is important to discern if the order-entry system can operate cosynchronistically with a quote system or chart service.

To protect the trader, backup systems are of particular importance, such as the ability to place an order over the telephone if there is a traffic jam on the "communications superhighway." It is important to determine if the on-line system has a customer service desk with a technician to walk the trader through concerns or to clear up problems.

Certainly, the background history of the order-entry system is important. It's better for someone else to have worked out the bugs in a program than for the trader to be exposed to the guinea pig process.

Russell can be reached at: www.pfgbest.com or at (800) 826-8035.

STEPHAN BENGER

Look Out, Chicago, Here Comes the Guru

Stephan Benger is chairman of PMB. While Stephan and I don't always agree, his predictions on Chicago markets are positively bone-chilling.

Neal: Stephan, how important will the Chicago markets be in the year ahead?

Stephan: The Chicago markets will definitely face a diminishing importance in the global marketplace. The concentration process within Europe will strengthen the appeal of the European exchanges. Due to the introduction of the Euro and the underlying principles behind it, some of the European derivatives traders who only, or mainly, traded U.S. markets will now increase the allocation of their portfolios into Europe. We are already experiencing this phenomenon within our firm; some of our bigger customers are increasingly focusing on European markets and decreasing their U.S. derivative exposure.

Neal: How would you contrast the trading styles of European and Chicago traders?

Stephan: Interestingly, one of the main differences between Europe and the U.S. is that there are more computerized exchanges in Europe. The biggest European exchange, Eurex (formerly DTB and Soffex) is electronic; LIFFE is getting its electronic trading platform off the ground in the first quarter of 1999; and most of the smaller European futures exchanges are electronic. I believe that one reason our customers are currently increasing their trading exposure in Europe is the transparency of electronic futures markets and the inherent fairness of such a system. Once an electronically traded market maintains a daily volume of trades so that it can be called liquid, the customer seems to prefer it over the open-outcry exchanges. I believe that the main reason these customers prefer to trade electronically is the instant fill they get out of an electronic exchange. This brings us to the concept of electronically accessing an exchange, bypassing the human interface and being filled on a market order within a second. This is only possible on an electronic exchange and really should be the reason why you want to trade electronically.

Comment: If Stephan is correct, trading Chicago style may be a legacy of the 1900s. I hope not. However, it is up to the leadership of the exchanges to answer that question.

Stephan Benger can be reached at (312) 407-6000. His Web site is www.pmb.com.

Pit Stops

Barry J. Lind, Who Knows Trading Chicago Style Better Than Anyone

Barry J. Lind, Lind-Waldock's chairman, is one of the most notable success stories in the futures industry. He first began trading in 1962. Three years later, he had developed enough public business to open his own firm. From his earliest days of membership, Mr. Lind has been active as both a trader and a leader of the Chicago Mercantile Exchange (CME) and later as a major contributor in shaping response to critical futures industry issues. Since it was first published in 1969, *Method Trading*, written by Mr. Lind, has grown in popularity with both public and professional traders. It has been translated into several languages. Over 100,000 copies are in circulation. The following questions are a follow-up to method trading.

Neal: Classic charting techniques have been at the forefront of trading for a long time here in Chicago. Are they still valid in light of system trading and 24-hour markets?

Barry: Charting techniques are still the same. But some techniques work in some markets, and some work in others. And what works today may not work in three months or six months. Sometimes I buy every breakout and sometimes I won't buy any. Charts are just a tool, not the be-all and end-all.

Neal: What are some of your favorite patterns when it comes to trading?

Barry: I'm a channel trader, whether long-term or for just a few minutes. If I'm trading short-term, I'm strictly technical. For the longer term, I'll get some opinions about the fundamentals. If the fundamental information matches the technical analysis, I may take a bigger position than I would ordinarily.

Neal: So, knowing the fundamentals makes you feel more comfortable?

Barry: Yes.

Neal: Do you have a Web site where traders can get more info?

Barry: Yes: www.lind-waldock.com.

Pit Stops

Talpx Spells Lumber

What is the future of Chicago-style trading? Well, look out. Here comes Talpx. This is a unique cash lumber exchange located at 303 W. Madison. There are no pits, market makers, scalpers, spreaders, or options.

The traders are the big players in the forestry business. The power of this virtual exchange is the fact that they tie the Internet and trading software together in a closed-end system. Bids and offers are displayed real-time, and delivery does take place. No speculators please. No running stops here.

If the idea takes off, they plan to market the concept worldwide. As they say in Chicago, this could be big . . . really big.

Talpx can be contacted at (312) 424-0334; Fax: (312) 424-0470.

OPTIMA

Chicago traders do not enter the pit with blank minds. They have access to reports that keep them informed during the trading day. Very few people know about Optima, which contains information compiled by a team of technicians and analysts.

The following sample is just a partial representation of the Optima report, which, in its entirety, provides detailed, comprehensive coverage of the markets and the factors that influence them. Optima comes out daily. Though dated, this sampling will give you the scope of the knowledge available to Chicago-style traders. If you have any questions regarding this report, call Optima Investment Research directly at (312) 427-3616 or e-mail Optima at www.oir.com or at www.optimainvestor.com.

Optima INVESTMENT RESEARCH

INTERNATIONAL Financial Comment

Monday 1/4/99—Americas Comment—The US markets today will focus on (1) today's release of the US Dec Purchasing Managers index, (2) the US credit market which opens the New Year with the focus on the strength of the US economy and whether the worst of the global financial crisis has passed or whether additional surprises may be in store, (3) US stock market which continues to trade at extraordinarily high valuation levels with a focus on speculative Internet stocks, (4) the FX market which enters a new paradigm this week as the marketplace waits to see whether the European Central Bank will follow in the Bundesbank's footsteps as a hawkish central bank or whether the ECB will follow a softer policy due to political pressure from the myriad of European political factions that will seek to influence the Bank, and (5) the CRB index which settled slightly mildly stronger last Thursday.

This week's US economic calendar is fairly busy with the key reports including today's Dec NAPM report and Friday's Dec unemployment report. Tomorrow brings Nov construction spending and the weekly retailer sales surveys. Wednesday brings Nov new home sales. Thursday brings Nov factory orders and Dec same-store retail chain sales reports. Friday brings the Dec unemployment report and Nov wholesale trade report.

The European markets will be closely watching for any glitches related to the start of euro trading today. The British markets are focussed on the BOE's MPC meeting set for Wednesday and Thursday. The Japanese markets are focussed on the sharp rise in JGB yields that has occurred in the past month and whether the Obuchi government will be able to finalize a coalition government with the Liberal Democratic Party. That coalition is likely to increase pressure for more stimulus measures.

Markets hope for resolution of Clinton impeachment situation by the end of January—The US markets will also focus on the Clinton impeachment situation. Senate Republican leaders are trying to find a graceful exit strategy given that there aren't enough votes in the Senate for a 2/3 conviction vote. The Senate has little stomach for a full trial that would likely include calling witnesses such as Monica Lewinsky. Therefore, the focus is on how to construct a procedure that leads to censure. The only real controversy is how badly to embarrass the President with the start of a trial before the censure measure comes to a vote. As far as the markets are concerned, the whole Clinton-Lewinsky scandal seems destined to fade away in the next month or so. However, the markets will still keep a close eye on the situation in the event that hard-line Republicans are able to take control of the process as they were able to in the House.

NAPM index is expected to show moderate gain but remain below 50—Today's US Dec NAPM index is expected to show a

+0.7 point increase to 47.5%, reversing about 1/2 of the −1.5 point plunge seen in Nov. Still, a reading below 50% would continue to point to a contraction in US manufacturing sector, albeit at a slower pace than in Nov. Expectations for a small rebound in the NAPM index stem from the Dec Philadelphia Fed index which showed a +10.3 point jump to −3.8, as well as the gains in both the Dec Chicago and NY-area manufacturing indexes released last Friday. As usual, the markets will key on the employment, price and new export orders sub-indexes of the overall report. In Nov, the employment index slipped by −0.1 point to 44.9%, holding just above July's 3-1/2 year low of 44.4%. The price index in Nov fell by −0.8 points to 35.0%, holding just above Sep's 49-year low of 34.4%. The new export orders edged +0.9 points higher in Nov to 42.9%, holding under the 50% mark for the 11th straight month.

US initial unemployment claims surge in the latest week— Initial unemployment claims rocketed +79,000 workers higher to 368,000 in the week ended Dec 26th. That was far above expectations for a rebound to 310,000 workers. The previous week's report was revised a bit higher to 289,000 workers from the earlier report of 287,000 workers. The +79,000 worker jump in claims marked the sharpest increase in the series in 6-1/ 2 years. Moreover, that left the series at a new 5-1/2 month high, just below the peak of 394,000 workers seen in the weeks ended June 27th and July 4th (at the height of the impact of the GM strikes and the annual re-tooling effort among auto makers). The 4-week moving average jumped by +13,500 workers to a new 5-month high of 321,250 workers.

In the week ended Dec 19th, the number of continuing claims climbed by +17,000 workers to 2.228 million. The 4-week moving average, however, fell by −15,500 workers to 2.234 million workers.

Last Thursday's initial unemployment claims report certainly raised some eyebrows in the financial markets, as it has for 3 straight weeks. First, the markets watched the plunge in claims to below the 300,000 worker mark to the 8-1/2 month low of 289,000 workers in the week ended Dec 19th. Now, the markets is watching the amazing rebound in the series to a 5-1/2 month high.

This volatility stems largely from the usual seasonal adjustment snafus that crop up through the holiday season and into the early part of January. Moreover, those problems were probably exacerbated in the latest week by the impact of severe winter storms in the Pacific Northwest (flooding) and the Southeast (ice). Therefore, the markets will likely overlook the initial claims series which has never been a very reliable indicator of the strength in the US labor market.

US Dec APICS Business Outlook Index edges lower—The Dec APICS Business Outlook Index slipped by −0.9 points to 47.6. APICS said that the Dec index pointed to "sluggish but positive growth in manufacturing activity during the first quarter of 1999." The future component fell by −1.3 points to 49.1, while the current component slipped by −0.5 points to 41.1.

All in all, the sluggish readings in the Dec APICS index are in line with expectations for continued softness in the US manufacturing sector. That, along with the export industries, have been the hardest hit by the impact of the Asian crisis and the lingering impact of the surge in the dollar seen from the spring of 1995 through the first half of this year.

US Dec regional Purchasing Managers indexes are mixed—The Dec Chicago-area Purchasing Managers index climbed by +0.7 points to 50.9%. That pointed to a small acceleration in the region's manufacturing activity. Strength in the headline index stemmed from gains in the production, order backlog, and inventories sub-indexes. However, the prices-paid, employment, and supplier deliveries indexes all fell, while the new orders index held steady.

Specifically, the prices paid index plunged by −9.5 points to a new 49-1/2 year low of 34.1%. That drop points to plunging input prices and should reinforce the slide seen in the CRB index in recent months. The employment index plunged by −7.8 points to a 2-1/2 year low of 44.4%.

The weakness in the employment index, as well as the strength in inventories (+10.4 points to a new 2-year high of 58.4%), overshadowed to some extent the headline strength in the overall Dec Chicago Purchasing index. The softness in hiring and the jump in inventories point to weakness in the region's manufacturing activity down the road.

The Dec NY-area Purchasing Managers index climbed by +6.8 points to 63.2%. That pointed to a sharp acceleration in the region's overall business activity. However, the strength in the headline index stemmed solely from a +10.3 point jump in the non-manufacturing index to a very strong reading of 67.4%. The manufacturing index, however, plunged by –24.2 points to 25.8%, thereby pointing to a sharp contraction in factory activity. Looking ahead, the outlook index (which looks forward over the coming 6 months) climbed by +7.0 points to a very strong 65.6%.

The mixed performances of the NY and Chicago-area Purchasing Managers reports masked some underlying softness. In the NY index, that softness was seen in the plunge in the manufacturing index to 25.8%. In the Chicago index, that softness was seen in the slide in hiring and the sudden build-up in inventories. That should bolster expectations for further weakness in manufacturing activity down the road and fuel hopes for further Fed easing if such weakness spreads into the key non-manufacturing sectors of the economy.

US Interest Rates—US credit market settles a bit softer in thin year-end trade—March T-bonds last Thursday spiked lower early in the shortened session and then rebounded upward to finally settle a bit weaker. **Futures closes:** USH99 –0-04 at 127-25; TYH99 –0-01 at 119-05; FVH99 –0-005 at 113-110; TUH99 +0-007 at 105-245; TBH99 –.005 at 95.765; EDM99 –.0100 at 95.0900. **Cash closes** (3PM NY): cash 30-yr –0-02 at 102-12; cash 30-yr yield +.004 at 5.094; cash 10-yr unch at 100-25; cash 10-yr yield unch at 4.651; cash 5-yr +0-01 at 98-25; cash 5-yr yield –.007 at 4.532; cash 2-yr +0-035 at 100-065; cash 2-yr yield –.069 at 4.494; 3-mo T-bill –.049 at 4.381.

March T-bonds last Thursday consolidated above the 8-week low of 125-26 (12/24/98) where they sold off by 5-06/32 points from the 2-1/2 month high of 131-00 (12/10/98). The cash 30-year bond yield last Thursday consolidated below the 6-week high of 5.233% (12/24/98) where it rebounded by a total of 30.8 bp from the Dec 11th 2-1/2 month low of 4.925% (matching the Oct 16th low). June Euros last Thursday held above the 3-1/2 month low of 94.93 (12/24/98) where they sold off by a total of 96.0 bp from the contract high of 95.89.

Bearish factors included (1) the plunge in the dollar, (2) long liquidation pressures following last week's brief rebound, (3) some long-term concerns about the advent of the euro and any subsequent asset reallocation, (4) supply pressures ahead of Wednesday's 10-year indexed bond auction and the expected flood of corporate supply to start the year, and (5) some carry-over pressure following the tumble in March JGBs which kept alive concerns about Japanese Treasury sales. **Bullish factors** included (1) Thursday's sharp sell-off in US stock prices, and (2) the underlying weakness seen in last Thursday's regional Purchasing Managers indexes.

The US credit market begins the New Year with relative stability on the global crisis front, continued strength in the US economy, and a high-flying stock market. This combination of events led the Fed at its November FOMC meeting to shift back to a neutral policy from its former bias toward easing. The release of the Nov FOMC meeting minutes prompted the market to significantly downgrade the chances for another Fed easing any time soon.

The shift in the market's outlook regarding the Fed is plainly visible in the fed funds futures curve which flattened dramatically in the past 2 weeks. The Feb contract last Thursday closed at 95.28, thereby pricing in a 4.72% funds rate or no chance of an easing at the FOMC's next meeting on Feb 2-3. The April contract settled at 95.33, pricing in a 4.67% funds rate or about a 30% chance of a 25 bp easing at the March 30th meeting. The June contract settled at 95.35, thereby pricing in a 4.65% funds rate or about a 40% chance of a 25 bp easing by mid-year.

Despite the Fed's neutral policy, the credit market will be searching for signs of broad-based weakness in the US economy. Economic growth this year is expected to slow from the +3.7% pace seen through the first 3 quarters of 1998 (Q4 GDP growth is expected at +3.5-4.0%), but that slowdown is not expected to be seen in the economic data for at least another 1-2 months. In fact, the December data that will begin emerging this week is expected to be strong and further foreclose any chance of a near-term Fed easing. The US credit market may therefore be left to tread water over the near-term, waiting for new developments on the US stock market, the global crisis, or the US economy.

Fed expected to conduct another supplemental system repo—The Fed today will likely conduct another supplementary repo to stay on top of its hefty holiday-related add need of about $10-12 bln in the new current 2-week period that began last Thursday. Moreover, the Fed will likely need to replace the two repos that expire today, i.e., last Thursday's fixed $5.175 billion 4-day system repo and last Monday's $6.059 billion fixed 7-day system repo. The Fed is currently facing a huge add need of about $20 billion but that should begin to taper off later this week. The add need will quickly decline in coming weeks and could even revert to a small drain need in mid to late January.

Outstanding repos include two repos that expire tomorrow (the fixed $4.727 billion 15-day system repo and last Tuesday's $2.805 billion fixed 7-day system repo), last Thursday's fixed $3.850 billion 6-day system repo that expires on Wednesday, the fixed $2.710 billion 30-day system repo that expires on Friday, the fixed $3.150 billion 45-day system repo that expires on Jan 21st, and the fixed $2.0 billion 41-day system repo that expires on Jan 27th. Those operations total a whopping $19.242 billion. Last Thursday's dual 4-day and 6-day system repos were conducted with the funds rate trading at 5-1/2%, well above the 4-3/4% funds rate target. That upward pressure was tied to the Fed's underlying add need, as well as end-of-year demand for reserves and liquidity.

Money supply aggregates surge in the latest week and M2 growth hits new 11-3/4 year high of +9.4%—All 3 money supply aggregates posted strong gains in the week ended Dec 21st: M1 +$14.9 billion, M2 +$18.7 bln, and M3 +$15.4 billion. Year-on-year growth in the widely-watched M2 aggregate accelerated to +9.3% from the previous week's +9.2% y/y gain. That marked the strongest increase in M2 growth in 11-3/4 years.

US Stock Market—The US stock market opened little changed last Thursday, traded lower for most of the session, and then surged into the close to finish mixed. Settlements: Dow Industrials −93.21 at 9181.43, DJH99 −75 at 9265, Dow Utilities +1.38 at 312.30, OEX −3.30 at 604.03, S&P 500 −2.70 at 1229.23, SPH99 +3.40 at 1245.50, NASDAQ Composite +25.74 at 2192.69, and the Russell 2000 +10.05 at 421.96.

The Dow fell −1.0% last Thursday followed by the S&P 500 down −0.2%. Meanwhile, the Russell 2000 jumped +2.4% and the NASDAQ rose +1.2% on the day. For the month of December, the NASDAQ surged +12.5%, the Russell 2000 rose +6.1%, the S&P 500 gained +5.6%, and the Dow edged up +0.7%. During 1998, the NASDAQ rocketed +39.1%, the S&P 500 advanced +26.7%, and the Dow increased +16.1%. The Russell 2000 lagged badly with a −3.5% loss, but recovered from the −30.5% year-to-date loss that the index suffered on its October 8th 2-3/4 year low.

Stock market breadth was strongly bullish last Thursday with advancing issues (2,315) leading declining issues (781) by a 3 to 1 margin. Volume for last Thursday's NYSE session was 639 million shares with declining volume accounting for 30% of the total. The percentage of NYSE stocks above their 200-day moving averages remained at a 5-month high of 38%. On September 1st, the percentage posted a 7-1/3 year low of 14% where it was down sharply from April's reading of 68%. The number of shares posting new 52-week highs (407) exceeded the number posting new 52-week lows (283).

Bullish factors included (1) a surge in small-cap issues ahead of the seasonally-favorable month of January, (2) upward momentum initiated by year-end purchases over the last 2-weeks, (3) a resumption of the euphoria for Internet issues, (4) recent indications that individual investors are putting money back into the stock market after several weeks of withdrawals.

Bearish factors included (1) profit taking in the large-cap issues, (2) a decline in telephone shares as Bell Atlantic was reported in talks to purchase AirTouch, (3) valuation concerns with the S&P 500's P/E ratio touching an all-time high of 31.9 on Dec 23rd (more than twice its long-term historical average), and (4) a narrowing of the market's breadth in December as the majority of the gains were confined to a number of high-tech stocks.

At the top of the most active list on a whopping 101.31 million shares was **Amoco** (+9.4%). The oil company dropped sharply last Wednesday as the approval of the $61.7 bln purchase by British Petroleum will result in the company falling out of the S&P 500 index. However, global investors realized that the merger puts Amoco into the FTSE-100 and money managers tracking the UK index must acquire the shares. **America Online** (+5.2%) was the second most active issue on 39.82 million shares as the hoopla surrounding its inclusion in the S&P 500 index last Thursday proved strongly positive. **Compuware** (+1.6%) rose on 20.40 million shares and posted a fresh 52-week high. Last Wednesday, *Fortune* named Compuware one of the 100 best companies to work for in America.

Of the S&P 500's 89 sub-indexes, 47 closed higher last Thursday while 41 closed lower. Market breadth was bullish with 301 of the S&P 500 stocks closing lower while 183 rose. On a capitalization weighted basis, the financial sub-index (−2.05%) was the worst performing group in the S&P 500 index as **Citigroup** (−1-1/16), **Fannie Mae** (−1-9/16), and **Morgan Stanley Dean Witter** (−2-3/16) all fell. Although financial companies expect another busy year in 1999, investors are cautious about the ability of the US securities industry to place more than the record of $1.82 trillion in securities set in 1998. The money center bank sub-index (−2.55%) was the second poorest performing group followed by the telephone sub-index (−1.01%) in the third slot.

Of the 30 stocks in the Dow Jones Industrial Average, 22 closed lower last Thursday while 88 closed higher. **American Express** led the Dow lower last Thursday with a −2-9/16 point loss. Although 1998 was a banner year for credit card companies, American Express is also saddled with weaker travel-related businesses. CardWeb reported that consumers spent $83 bln during the 1998 holiday season compared to $74.5 bln in 1997. **Dupont** was the second biggest decliner among Dow stocks (−2-3/8) as analysts note that the conglomerate is still in the process of spinning off Conoco. Conoco was purchased in 1981 and Dupont has now divested itself of 30% with the remainder expected to be jettisoned during 1999. The return derived from the Conoco sale has been negatively impacted by oil prices at 12-year lows.

On last Thursday's all-time high of 2200.63, the **NASDAQ Composite index** extended its 2-3/4 month rally from the 1-2/3 year low of 1357.09 (Oct 8) to a total of 843.54 points (62.2%). On last Wednesday's all-time high of 1244.93, the **S&P 500 index** extended its rally from its 1-year low of 923.32 (Oct 8) to a total of 321.61 points (34.8%). On its all-time high of 9380.20 (Nov 24), the **Dow Industrial** extended its upmove from its 1-year low of 7400.30 (Sep 1) to a total of 1,979.90 points (26.8%). On last Thursday's 4-1/2 month high of 421.98 the **Russell 2000** was up 118.11 points (38.9%) from its 2-2/3 year low of 303.87 (Oct 8). Also on last Thursday's high, the index retraced 63% of its 8-month, 188.41 point (38.3%) downmove from the all-time high of 492.28 (Apr 22).

Commodities—CRB closes higher as energy sector advances—The CRB index last Thursday closed +.51 points at 191.22 and held above the 21-year low at 187.89 posted on Dec 21st. Support exists at the 23-year low at 184.70 which was posted in 1977. Resistance exists at the Nov 30th 1-month high of 197.73. The CRB index dropped −2.1% in the month of December and −16.5% in 1998. The severe downmove in the CRB during 1998 was the largest on an annual basis since the −17.4% correction in 1981 which had followed the all-time high level posted during 1980 at 337.60.

The CRB index posted a 21-year low in 1998 despite record levels in the US stock market which has rallied 13 times over in the past 21 years. During 1998, crude oil posted a 12-year low, corn posted a 10-year low, lean hogs posted a 26-year low, cotton posted a 5-year low, and sugar posted an 11-year low. The theme for the commodity markets continues to be slack global demand due to the global financial crisis and excess supply in the production markets.

Closes: **Energy:** CLG99 +.30 at 12.05; HUG99 +.0070 at .3655; HOG99 +.0066 at .3428; NGG99 +.059 at 1.945. **Precious Metals:** GCG99 +1.1 at 289.2; SIH99 −1.5 at 502.0; PLJ99 +3.3 at 367.2. **Grains:** SH99 −0-6 at 541-2; SMH99 −2.40 at 139.40; BOH99 +.09 at 23.11; C H99 unch at 213-4; W H99 +0-2 at 276-2. **Livestock:** LCG99 +.05 at 60.52; FCF99 +.17 at 69.17; LHG99 −.60 at 32.65; PBG999 −.52 at 42.75. **Softs:** SBH99 −.02 at 7.86; KCH99 +.60 at 117.75; CCH99 +3. at 1379.; JOH99 −2.55 at 104.30. **Industrials:** CTH99 −.08 at 60.36; HGH99 +.30 at 67.20; LBF99 +3.10 at 305.60.

Feb natural gas was the CRB's biggest winner last Thursday as the contract rose +.059 to settle at 1.945. On last Monday's low at 1.770, natural gas tumbled −.850 (32.44%) from the Nov 9th 4-month high at 2.620. Natural gas rallied on the AGA storage report released after the close last Wednesday. The AGA report showed that natural gas storage fell −167 bcf w/w which was the highest level of withdrawals in two years. Weather forecasts call for below-normal temperatures through most of the nation this week. Heating demand is expected to be 22% above normal in the northern Midwest and also in New York and Boston.

Mar orange juice was the CRB's biggest negative contributor as the contract fell −2.55 cents to 104.30. On last Thursday's 3-month low at 103.50, orange juice dropped −17.50 cents from the Dec 7th 1-month high at 121.00. Orange juice was pressured by speculation that the table oranges damaged in the recent California freeze will be squeezed for orange juice. Under normal circumstances, 80% of California oranges are sold for table consumption. The Dec USDA supply forecast for the

Florida orange crop was unchanged compared to October at 190 mln boxes. The figure of 190 mln boxes would be −22% below last year's record harvest of 244 mln boxes.

Feb crude oil last Thursday rose +30 cents to close at $12.05 after posting a contract low of 10.75 on Dec 21st. On that low, crude oil plunged −2.20 dollars (16.98%) from the Dec 16th 1-1/4 month high at 12.95. US and UK jets returned fire upon an Iraqui missile site in response to a second anti-craft attack last week. Last Tuesday, API reported that crude oil inventories declined a bullish −2.4 mln barrels. Colder weather in the US is expected to help normalize demand which has dipped below average during the warm start to the winter heating season. Analysts have noted that budgets deficits in Saudi Arabia may prevent crude oil production cuts in the first half of 1999.

INDEX

ABOUT THE AUTHOR

Neil Weintraub has years of experience as a floor trader, Commodity Trading Advisor, and instructor at the Chicago Mercantile Exchange. Weintraub teaches his Pivot Point Analysis—an innovative day-trading method—to floor traders at the Chicago Mercantile Exchange. He wrote the bestselling *Tricks of the Floor Trader*.